**Decision
Processes
International**
"Leader in Critical Thinking"

418 Addison Place
Ridgewood, NJ 07450-4514
Tel.: (203) 454-1286
    1-800-336-7685
Fax: (203) 226-5802
E-mail: ted.gerber@dpi-ww.com

Ted Gerber
Partner

Argentina • Brazil • Canada • France • Germany • Hong Kong • Italy
Malaysia • Mexico • New Zealand • Portugal • Singapore • South Africa
Spain • Sweden • Switzerland • United Kingdom • United States

Strategy
PURE & SIMPLE

How To
Build Your
Own Strategy
and Achieve
Competitive
Supremacy

"**You need to have
supremacy of** *thinking*
**before you can achieve
supremacy of** *strategy.*"

– Michel Robert
Founder, Partner
Decision Processes International

Also by Michel Robert

The Strategist CEO
The Innovation Formula
Strategy Pure and Simple
Product Innovation Strategy Pure and Simple
Strategy Pure and Simple II
The Power of Strategic Thinking
e-Strategy Pure and Simple

Michel Robert is the founding partner of Decision Processes
International, a global management consulting firm which is
a pioneer in the field of Critical Thinking Processes. These
processes, such as Strategic Thinking, Strategic Product
Innovation and the Strategic Information Process, have
helped more than 500 companies to achieve supremacy
and transform the way they do business.

Additional books may be ordered from Decision Processes
International, 10 Bay Street, Westport, CT 06880.
Telephone: 1-800-336-7685 (in CT: 203-454-1286).
Fax: 203-226-5802.
Visit DPI on the Internet at www.decisionprocesses.com

Strategy
PURE & SIMPLE

How To
Build Your
Own Strategy
and Achieve
Competitive
Supremacy

Michel Robert

Founder – Partner
Decision Processes International

Published by

PPS

Poutray, Pekar, Stella, Inc.
Norwalk.CT

Robert, Michel
    Strategy pure and simple. / Michel Robert

    ISBN 0-9709985-1-1
    1. Strategic Planning – United States
2. Competition   3. Success in Business – United States
I. Title.

            Published by:

            PPS

    Poutray, Pekar, Stella, Inc.
            Norwalk, CT
        203-853-4000

        1 2 3 4 5 6 7 8 9 0

ISBN 0-9709985-1-1

Books are available from Decision Processes International,
10 Bay Street, Westport, CT 06880, 1-800-336-7685,
(in CT 203-454-1286), fax: 203-226-5802.
Internet: www.decisionprocesses.com

Although the author has thoroughly researched all sources to ensure the
accuracy and completeness of the information contained in this book we
assume no responsibility for errors, inaccuracies, omissions and any other
inconsistency herein. Any slights against people or organizations are
unintentional.

Edited by William D. Poutray
Book jacket design by Dawn Smeraglino
Typesetting by Mary Pike and Dawn Smeraglino

To my wife Ellie, my best critic, for enduring my writing books on our honeymoon and our vacations. And to my daughters, Emma and Samantha, who I hope will be inspired to realize that achievement in life is totally unrelated to one's origin.

Contents

Preface

Our firm, Decision Processes International, has been involved in the field of strategy for over twenty-five years. During this span of time, we have seen a multitude of so-called strategy consultants and strategic concepts come and go faster than the latest seasonal clothing fad.

To mention just a few that have come and gone since 1975, the following are some of the concepts that have landed on the strategic scrapheap.

- The concept of *Stars, Dogs, and Cash Cows* espoused by the Boston Consulting Group

- The *Diversified Portfolio* concept, also espoused by the Boston Consulting Group in the 1970s

- The *"S" curve theory* espoused by McKinsey

- The *Value Chain* concept espoused by Michael Porter and the Monitor Group

- The *Undiversification of Diversified Portfolios* concept, again espoused by the Boston Consulting Group in the 1980s

- The concept of *Strategic Intent* espoused by Gary Hamel in the mid-1980s

- The concept of *Raising The Bar* as espoused by Jack Welch of General Electric

- The concept of *Balanced Scorecard* espoused by Nathan Kaplan

Many of these concepts were so "sexy" that they seduced many intelligent CEOs and their executive teams into using them, only to find out sometime later that they were conceptually flawed. They were flawed because the concepts had not been validated in the real world. They emerged from books written by business school professors who studied firms from the "outside" and attempted to recreate the magic recipes that these firms were following without ever speaking to anyone at these companies. They then published a book around their so-called "findings."

At DPI, we believe that the reason our concepts of *Strategic Thinking,* which we first marketed in 1980, have withstood the test of time is that they were developed in a very different manner. They were developed by participating in *real strategy* meetings conducted by *real* CEOs running *real* companies. In other words, our concepts originated from the "war rooms" of some of the world's leading corporations and have been validated with more than four hundred other corporations over more than twenty years.

Our *Strategic Thinking Process,* first introduced in 1980, contains several unique and proprietary concepts, such as:

- The concept that intelligent managers, not consultants, are best qualified to create strategy

- The concept of a singular Driving Force at the root of a company's strategy

- The concept of Areas of Excellence required to assure the success of a strategy

- The concept that companies compete, not business units

- The concept of Strategic Leveraging

- The concept of managing your competitor's strategy to your advantage

- The concept of controlling the "sandbox"

- The concept of not simply changing the rules, but changing the game itself

- The concept of pre-empting a "stealth" competitor

These have not only stood the test of time, but have become more robust as they have been "put to the test" around the world by the executive teams of these four hundred major corporations.

Our work with our clients also allows us to detect emerging concepts *before* they become "mainstream" and before business school professors become aware of them.

This book is about such an event. Since 1980, we have counseled our clients that *"significant shifts in market share occur, not by imitating a competitor's strategy, but by developing a strategy that changes the rules of play."* This concept has worked brilliantly for many of our clients.

The methodology we use to help them achieve these results is a proprietary Critical Thinking Process called *Strategic Thinking.* It enables a management team to objectively assess its present business and, together, forge a new vision of their future business concept that they can all agree upon and implement. It is *not* about a consultant telling people what to do. It *is* about harnessing the experience, intellect, and creativity of the people who know the business best – its management team.

The results of this process have been surprisingly consistent over the years – consensus, commitment, effective implementation, and, most importantly, increased growth and profitability.

During this period, I have authored eleven books that contain interviews with over fifty CEOs of our client organizations who all attest to these results.

Recently, however, we have noticed a number of changes happening in the world of business that have convinced us that merely changing the rules of play will not be enough to win in the future. Our thesis, as described in the remainder of this book, is that companies that aspire to attain *competitive supremacy* in the future will have to *change the very nature of the game itself.*

No longer will it be enough to change the rules. It will become imperative to *reinvent the game itself,* thus enabling a company to force its competitors to play this new game according to daunting new rules.

This is what this book is all about.

Good reading!

Michel Robert

1

Strategic Gridlock: How to Overcome the Six Situations That Can Derail a CEO's Strategy

"Winning companies will be those that out-think, not out-muscle, their competitors."

"It's easy to develop a strategy; it's the *implementation* that's difficult." This is a statement we have frequently heard over the years. Our own experience shows that the *formulation* of a strategy by traditional strategic planning methods is, at best, difficult and complicated. The very method by which it is created almost guarantees inconsistent, difficult deployment because the "implementors" either don't understand it or don't agree with it. Often these plans are created by a planning group, or worse, a consultant, and viewed as irrelevant or alien. Because of this, many CEOs have to invest an inordinate amount of their time getting people to implement their strategies. The following are some of the situations CEOs often encounter.

> **Situation #1: People cannot implement what they don't know.**

The Strategy Is Implicit And Not Explicit

In too many organizations, the strategy of the company is implicit and resides solely in the head of the chief executive. Most chief executives have a strategy. However, they often have great difficulty articulating it to the people around them in words that allow them to make consistent and intelligent decisions on behalf of the company.

One senior executive of a *Fortune 500* company once said to us, "The reason I have difficulty implementing my CEO's strategy is because I don't know what it is!"

Because many CEOs have difficulty verbalizing their strategies, most people are placed in the position of having to "guess" what the strategy is, and they may guess wrong as often as they guess right. Or else they learn what the strategy is over time by the nature of the decisions they recommend, which are either accepted or rejected. Gradually, a subordinate learns where the line of demarcation is between the things that are permitted by the strategy and those that are not. This is called *strategy by groping.* This occurs because the strategy becomes clear or explicit only over a long period of time, during which people may have spent too much time pursuing and implementing activities that did not fit, while neglecting opportunities that represented a better strategic fit. Worse, the strategy may never become clear, or may be badly misinterpreted by people making an earnest effort to figure it out.

As one of our CEO clients once told us after our initial session: "I was astonished that our senior management group had no concept of our strategy and disagreed with it once they learned of it."

The Strategy Is Developed In Isolation

A second reason the strategy may not be implemented properly is that it was developed by the CEO in isolation. This is a natural enough tendency, since a CEO's job *is* strategy. Furthermore, most subordinates have no experience *thinking strategically*, so there is no inclination, or framework, to involve others.

Many CEOs have a strategy, but their key people are not involved in the *process*, and therefore have no ownership. In such a case, subordinates usually do not understand the rationale behind the strategy and will spend more time questioning it, or trying to figure out where they fit, than implementing it. The CEO becomes more and more impatient as subordinates question his logic more and more often. The CEO, on the other hand, can't comprehend why his people are not executing what, to him, is a simple strategy.

> **Situation #2: People don't implement properly what they don't understand!**

Some CEOs might involve one or two people in the formulation of the strategy. This is better than doing it alone but is still not good enough. The *entire* management team must be involved in order to achieve accurate understanding and proper execution. This cannot be accomplished simply by "going offsite" with this group to discuss the strategy. A methodology, or process, is needed to guide the discussion and keep it "strategic," not operational. This is the basis of the *Strategic Thinking Process* we will unfold for you later in this book. Involvement by senior managers in the basic strategic decisions is the most effective way to create a strategy that not only looks good on paper, but actually gets implemented.

As John Davis, President of American Saw and Manufacturing Company, and a DPI client, put it:

> "I think that, too often, strategies are made in a vacuum. The management is given a copy of the plan and asked to imple-

ment it. I'm not sure they buy into that kind of plan. But, by going through the *Strategic Thinking Process*, there's a lot of debate and everyone sees the reasons why certain Critical Issues surface and things get done much more quickly."

The Strategy Is Developed By An Outside Consultant

The worst of all strategic crimes and the "kiss of death" for any strategy – even a good one – is to have an outside consultant develop your strategy. No outside consultant has the right to set the direction of your organization or knows as much about the business and the environment it is facing as your own people. Most strategies developed by outside consultants end up in the wastepaper basket for two reasons:

1. Everyone can quickly tear the conclusions apart because they are not based on an intimate knowledge of the company, the business, or the industry.

2. There is no commitment to that strategy by senior management because it is not *their* strategy.

Experience has shown that almost any strategy will work to some degree, unless it is completely invalidated by negative environmental factors. Experience has also shown, however, that no strategy will work as well as it should if a couple or a few members of senior management are not committed to that strategy. In effect, if total commitment is not present, those uncommitted to the strategy will, at best, implement it half-heartedly and, at worst, on a day-to-day basis, do everything in their power to prove it wrong.

As another CEO client, Kurt Weidenhaupt of American Precision Industries, said:

"I have been exposed to McKinsey, Boston Consulting Group, and Bain. They are all very capable and I'm sure their approach is very sound. The only problem is their product is not of the people, by the people, through the people. It's not owned by the people who later have to live with it. When the strategy is developed by an outside third party, it is an alien product, no matter how well it relates to the company."

Situation #3: People don't implement what they are not committed to.

In order to obtain commitment, key managers must be involved at each step of the process so that their views are heard and discussed. Participation, although it may seem time-consuming, builds commitment and, in our experience, saves exponentially more time on the deployment end of the equation. Key managers buy into the strategy because they helped construct it. It is as much their strategy as the CEO's.

Many CEOs have used our process knowing the outcome in advance. They did so anyway, using it as a tool to tap the advice and knowledge of their people and to obtain commitment to the conclusions, so that implementation of the strategy can then proceed expeditiously. Still others, thinking they knew what the outcome would be, discovered new ideas or flaws in their assumptions that would have caused difficulties down the road. By gathering the collective knowledge of key people, such ideas can be evaluated and problems can be flushed out and dealt with before they happen.

Three of our CEO clients expressed it this way:

> "I think the process increases management's understanding. I could probably have relayed that kind of thinking to that same group by other means, but not as successfully or in that same condensed timeframe."

> "My belief is that the best strategy is the one that people believe in, because then they are *driven* to achieve it. You can have the best strategy on paper, but if nobody is driven to achieve it, you don't succeed. I believe that to be successful, your key people must be part of the process."

> "The DPI process brings you to consensus on the Critical Issues that need to be addressed. In a very short timeframe, you can get the whole management team there."

Situation #4: Operational people are not trained to be
good strategic thinkers.

As noted earlier, most people working in organizations
spend their entire careers dealing exclusively with operational issues; they are not good strategic thinkers. With few
exceptions, we have found that only the CEO or the general
manager sees the "big picture" and views the business and
its environment in strategic terms. There usually is only one
strategist in any organization and that is the CEO. Most
managers are so engrossed in operational activity that they
have not developed the skill of thinking *strategically*.
Therefore, they have difficulty coping with strategic issues,
especially if these are sprung on them out of the blue at a
"retreat." "The problem," says Milton Lauenstein in an article
in the *Journal of Business Strategy*, "is that many executives
have only the fuzziest notion of the functions of strategy
formulation." This is why a process that guides the management team through these strategic issues is essential.
Expecting your operational people to suddenly become
strategists without such a tool will create more problems
than it solves. On the flip side, given such a process, most
senior managers will surprise you with their ability to think
strategically and creatively once they have the framework,
permission, and opportunity to do it.

Situation #5: Key subordinates may simply not understand the difference between strategic and operational
thinking.

People will implement a strategy more effectively if they
understand the difference between a strategic process and
either long-range or operational planning. They also need to
be able to distinguish between strategic and operational
issues. Participation in a clearly *strategic* process is an eye-
opener for most managers. Most have never participated in
a strategy session, or if they have, they find that they have
primarily dealt with operational issues, and so never learn
the difference.

> Situation #6: People give up on a strategy whose implications have not been anticipated.

The Critical Issues Are Not Identified

One aspect of strategy is its formulation. Another is thinking through its implications. Most strategic planning systems we have seen used in organizations don't encourage people to think through the implications of their strategy. As a result, they end up reacting to these events as they are encountered and many people start losing faith in the strategy. As a senior vice president of a major organization put it, "There were so many things I did not understand in the CEO's strategy, I gave up trying to implement it." Every strategy, especially if it represents a change of direction, has implications.

A good strategic process should help management identify, anticipate, and effectively manage the strategy's implications on the company's products, markets, customers, organization structure, personnel, and culture.

Process And Content

What is a process and how does it work? In every strategy session that we facilitate, there are always two dynamics at work, namely *process* and *content*. Content is information or knowledge that is company- or industry-specific. Telephone company executives know a lot about cables, switch gears, PBXs, analog or digital devices, and transmission. They know all this "content" because they were "brought up" in the industry and that is the content that is specific to that industry. It is piece and parcel of their lexicon.

Executives at 3M or Caterpillar, however, know nothing about analog or digital devices or switch gears but they do know a lot about their own "content." At 3M, all executives at the top have degrees in chemistry or chemical engineering and, as a result, can talk for hours about polymer chemistry and its use in coating and abrasive applications. Such is their world.

At Caterpillar, executives can mesmerize you for hours talking about metallurgy, welding, payloads, diesel horsepower, and their ability to "cut iron" better than anyone else. This is their "content" . . . and their comfort zone.

In order to climb the ladder in most companies one needs to be a "content expert." This is necessary in order to be able to manage your way through the day-to-day "content laden" operational issues. Most executives get to the top of their respective silos, or functional areas, because of their content expertise, and rightly so.

At the strategic level, which is *above* the silos, content expertise alone is not sufficient. In fact, too much content knowledge may be a major impediment to good strategic thinking. This is because strategic thinking is *process-based* rather than *content-based.* Operational management requires the skill of *analysis*, while strategic management requires the skill of *synthesis.*

Analysis is the ability to study content and put it into logical *quantitative* pieces. Synthesis is the ability to make rational decisions based on highly subjective, sometimes ambiguous or incomplete, pieces of data. Synthesis is highly *qualitative* in nature. Strategic thinking falls into this category. It is the ability to take subjective data and opinions and bring these into an *objective* forum where rational decisions about the future of the enterprise can be made. In order to achieve this outcome, a CEO must have a "critical thinking" process. Critical thinking is the rational approach to decision making. A "critical thinker" is able to assemble all available information, put it into perspective, and draw rational conclusions. This approach works especially well for groups of decision makers in that it organizes information, separates fact from myth, and enables groups to reach consensus, or agreement, on decisions objectively. Critical thinking is, essentially, applied common sense, and is easy for anyone to understand once the methodology is available.

Content Versus Process Consultants

A CEO who elects to seek outside assistance to help decide the future direction of the company is faced with having to choose between two very different types of consultants.

One is the "content" consultant. These are the traditional firms, such as McKinsey, Bain, Boston Consulting Group, Monitor, and many others. Their claim to fame is that they have "industry experts" who know their industry better than the client does. Their objective is to formulate a strategy *for* you since your people are not as knowledgeable as their "experts." In other words, they do it *for* you, or *to* you.

In our view, this form of consulting may be appropriate with regards to operational issues, but it is not appropriate to strategy and strategic direction. These firms are "content" consultants and they are selling content. Unfortunately, they sell the same content to all their clients in that industry. The best result is a "me-too" strategy that does not set you apart from your competitors and will never bring supremacy over them. You are, in our humble opinion, *outsourcing your thinking.*

A better service to a CEO and the management team is to bring them a critical thinking *process* and guide them through that process. However, it is *their* content going into the process and it is *their* content coming out. When the strategy has been constructed by the people who have the best content to offer and have a vital stake in the outcome, such a strategy gets implemented much more quickly and much more successfully than one that is imposed on them by an outside third party.

Laurie Dippenaar, CEO of FirstRand, South Africa's largest financial services firm, agreed after using our process:

> "What's affected us more than anything else is the fact that it systematically extracts the thinking and ideas from the executives' heads, rather than imposing the consultant's thinking. I think it almost *forces it out* of their heads. That obviously leads to the strategy being owned by the company, rather than by the consultant. I'm not just repeating what DPI says – it actually works that way."

The CEO As Process Leader

"Follow me!" T. E. Lawrence shouted to his Arab troops as he led his army's charge into battle.

Although the term "leadership" is frequently used to describe successful CEOs, few executives in business today can be considered true leaders. The litmus test for any leader is whether he or she will be followed, as Lawrence of Arabia was followed, by an army of people who were not even of his race or religion. For the followers to allow themselves to be led assumes their implicit belief in the leader's ability. Followers want to know *where* they are being led.

Many books have been written on leadership, but few have been able to describe it in comprehensive terms. Nor have they been able to describe the skill of leadership in any detail except to attribute it to a "trait of personality." John P. Kotter, in his 1988 book, *The Leadership Factor*, explained that leadership can be defined, analyzed, and learned. He also pointed out that it is not taught in business schools. Unfortunately, he did not articulate in his book *how* leadership skills can be acquired.

Jack Welch, former President and CEO of GE, described it this way in a *Business Week* interview:

> "A leader is someone who can develop a vision of what he or she wants their business, their unit, to do and be. Somebody who is able to articulate to the entire unit what the unit is and gain through a sharing of the discussion – listening and talking – an acceptance of that vision, and then can relentlessly drive implementation of that vision to a successful conclusion."

The flip side of this position was summed up by Roger Smith, former CEO of General Motors, in a *Fortune* interview. In explaining his failure to turn that company around more quickly, Smith cited the "inability to communicate his vision of General Motors earlier and more frequently" than he did.

Welch's definition of leadership is probably as close to the mark as any we could conjure up ourselves. However, hidden in this definition is the assumption that the CEO has mastered the skill of *strategic thinking*, the process used by a CEO to formulate, articulate, communicate, and successfully deploy a clear, concise, and explicit strategy for the organization.

A Fundamental Skill Of Leadership

Many CEOs are good strategic thinkers. The problem, however, is that they practice their skill by *osmosis* and are not
conscious of its various elements and steps. As a result, they
do not use the process systematically. They may also have
great difficulty transmitting their ability to their subordinates. The reason is simple. Whatever cannot be described
cannot be transferred.

Our experience, through twenty years of working with
management teams in many industries, suggests that most
people who surround a CEO are not strong strategic
thinkers themselves. Again, the reason is simple. As we have
said, since managers are so engrossed in operational activity, so isolated in their functional silos, they are not accustomed to thinking strategically. A CEO, therefore, may wish
to involve subordinates in a deliberate application of the
Strategic Thinking Process strictly for its educational value
for both the CEO and his or her subordinates.

Commented Bob Burgess, CEO of Pulte Homes:

> "The real benefit of going through this process is what hap-
> pens in the weeks and months that follow. It has caused us
> to raise the level of strategic thinking both in the field and at
> the corporate office."

The Role Of The CEO

There is only one person in any organization who can "drive"
the *Strategic Thinking Process* and that is the chief executive
of that organization. *Strategic thinking, then, must start with
the CEO. Strategic Thinking* is definitively a trickle-down
process and not a bubble-up one. It is a very interactive
process, but the CEO must be its owner. As such, the CEO
must show commitment to the process by participating in all
its phases and work sessions.

Because the process is highly interactive, it is not for the
fainthearted. The process invites discussion, debate, and
constructive provocation. Everyone, during its various phases,
has the opportunity to express his or her views, have these

challenged, and then challenge those of others. As a result, the process is ideal for CEOs who encourage frank, open discussion of issues and challenges and believe in the value of extracting the best thinking from those who know the company best – its management.

A CEO has two options available to get a strategy implemented. The first approach is *compliance.* Here, the CEO announces what the strategy is and how he or she expects it to be implemented. The CEO then assigns different tasks to different individuals. They, in turn, implement the strategy – or not – without questioning its rationale. In a world of increasing complexity, this approach has less and less appeal to more and more CEOs.

The second, and more effective, method is *commitment.* Here, key executives actively participate in developing the rationale behind the strategy and assist the CEO in crafting the strategy itself. In order to ensure widespread commitment to the strategy, most CEOs include the top two levels of management in the process. In the words of Milt Honea, CEO of NorAm Energy:

> "By using our own people and our own ideas, we have been able to achieve total buy-in by those responsible for implementing the strategy – our own team."

Total Immersion For A New CEO

When a new CEO joins a company, or rises up from the ranks to take the top job, the pressure to perform, particularly in a public company, begins immediately. In fact, a recent study by Burson Marsteller showed that, on average, a new CEO must prove his ability to produce results within five quarters. According to the study, he is expected to produce a strategic vision within eight months, increase the share price within nineteen months, and turn a company around within twenty-one months.

As anyone who has come into a company from the outside knows, the first few months are spent getting to know the key management people, the industry, customers, and so on.

We have found that going through the *Strategic Thinking*

Process early in one's tenure can greatly compress this learning period through total immersion.

Said our client, Kurt Wiedenhaupt, CEO of American Precision Industries:

> "This process can be used by any new CEO coming into a company or business he is not fully familiar with. In a very short period of time, you immerse yourself into this business. You get a deep understanding of the issues. You get a very good feeling for the players in your organization who are participating in this process. It took at least half a year out of my learning process."

Adds Brian Hayward, who had just become CEO of United Grain Growers:

> "We needed a process where we could all find a common direction. I didn't want to come in as a dictator and say, 'Okay, here's what we're going to do.' I had seen so much fragmentation and lack of unity, that even before I was officially in place I contacted DPI."

The Role Of The Process Facilitator

One role that the CEO should not attempt to play is that of *process facilitator*. One cannot have one foot in the process and one foot in the content. Attempting to guide the process while participating in the debate will give everyone the impression that the CEO is trying to manipulate the process to a predetermined conclusion. Therefore, it is wiser to have a third-party facilitator guide the process along.

Said Larry Smith, Managing Director of Castrol (U.K.):

> "I needed somebody to act as a controller or arbiter. I didn't want to dictate to the other management people what the strategy should be or dominate the process so it appeared to be my strategy and not theirs."

Adds Jesus Catania, Managing Director of Fagor Electro-domésticos:

> "A third-party facilitator who understands the process better than we do is a better judge of the quality of the answers and

ensures that we have not skipped any steps that might lead to wrong conclusions."

A facilitator is not a *moderator*. A moderator is a person who directs traffic as well as he or she can during a meeting, but without relying on a specific process. By contrast, a facilitator is a trained professional who comes to each meeting with a *structured* process, together with predesigned instruments that keep the discussion moving forward in a constructive manner toward a specific set of conclusions. The facilitator also keeps the process honest, balanced, and objective.

Heinrich Bossard, CEO of the Bossard Group, put it this way:

"DPI's methodology is process oriented without distortion of the content. DPI's way gave us the opportunity to develop our own strategy using their instruments *neutrally*, without bias toward a specific solution. They acted like a metronome. We had to play the piano, but they provided the metronome. They didn't try to impose any solutions. I watched out for that during the process. I would say the DPI facilitator managed it well."

The facilitator also prevents the individuals with the highest rank or loudest voice from dominating the discussion and distorting the conclusions. This includes the CEO. The CEO of a *Fortune 10* company said to me during one of our work sessions, "You know, Mike, you're the only one in this room who tells me to sit down and I do. No one else in this room would dare say that to me."

The Process Is The Focal Point

However talented our people may be as facilitators, we never forget that it is the *process* which allows executives that we work with to formulate a winning strategy.

In the rest of this book, we will flesh out the principles underlying the *Strategic Thinking Process* and, more importantly, the kinds of results that companies can expect to achieve when applying them.

At one time, it may have been enough to have a strategic plan on the shelf. No more. Only results count. It used to be enough to "be a player," or one of the competitors running with the pack. No more. It used to be enough to attempt to influence "the rules of play" in your market, a concept that we pioneered. Today we find that even that is not enough. Today, to achieve long-term performance, we have concluded that influencing or even changing the rules doesn't go far enough. It is necessary, and possible for almost any company, to devise a strategy that *changes the game*, leading to *supremacy over competitors*. This is made possible by the rapid pace of change and the many new avenues it opens up. This leads to new ideas for breaking away from the established game and "business as usual" and "we've always done it that way" thinking. That is what the remaining chapters will guide you through.

2

Competitive Supremacy: The Ultimate Goal of Strategy

"Supremacy, not adequacy, is the sole objective of a good strategy."

What do Intel, Wal-Mart, Home Depot, Microsoft, Dell, Apple, Oracle, Schwab, E-Trade, amazon.com, FedEx, Caterpillar, IBM, General Electric, Nokia, Progressive Insurance, Canon, Sony, Disney, and Southwest Airlines have in common? Let's try to answer this question using a process of elimination by first looking at what is *different* about each of them:

- They are in different industries.

- They have different products.

- They serve different customers and markets.

- They have different "modus operandi."

- They are headquartered in different countries.

- They cultivate different corporate cultures.

- They were conceived in different eras.

The list could go on *ad infinitum.* For example, another difference is that they have different CEOs. However, these different companies have, or at one point had, CEOs who had one trait in common. And that trait is a grasp of the concept of *competitive supremacy.* In other words, their goal was not to have a strategy that allowed their companies to compete "adequately," but rather a strategy that aimed at *supremacy* over their competitors. *Supremacy,* not *adequacy,* is the ultimate goal of strategy.

Supremacy: The Ultimate Goal Of Strategy

Supremacy over your competitors? What an arrogant position to which to aspire! Yet, whatever one may think about the role of competition, the ultimate measure of a successful strategy is not that it allows you to compete "adequately," a management philosophy preached by "best practices" strategy gurus for the last 30 years. Best practices, benchmarking, balanced scorecard are all techniques that lead to "imitation" strategies. The ultimate goal of strategy should not be to imitate competitors, but to strive toward making competitors much less relevant, or even *irrelevant.*

In fact, our view is that if you are obsessed with your competitors, it is probably because you have a "me-too" strategy that's not working and which should be given a "rethink." CEOs of winning companies have strategies that are *distinctive* and set them apart from their competitors. Their view of competitors is not to look sideways to see who is a "neck" ahead, but rather to periodically look *back* to ensure that the gap between them and their nearest competitor(s) is getting wider and wider. Competitive *supremacy*, not competitive adequacy, is the goal of astute CEOs. After all, history would have made short shrift of anyone named Alexander the Average or Frederick the Mediocre.

Changing The Rules Is No Longer Sufficient

How did the companies mentioned at the beginning of this chapter reach their elite positions of supremacy? The answer: by practicing a concept of strategy that we first introduced to our clients over twenty years ago – that the best strategy is not one that *imitates* your competitor, but rather, one that *changes the rules of play!*

Imitation may be the best form of flattery, but it is the worst form of strategy. You do not distance yourself from your competitors by cloning their strategies. You do so by crafting a strategy that changes the rules of play to the extent that it allows you to *manage that competitor's strategy* as well as your own. And that is exactly what each of the CEOs of the companies mentioned above had – a strategy that changed the rules of play.

The concept of *changing the rules of play* is one that has stood the test of time and we have many clients who have been very successful by formulating and deploying such strategies. However, in view of the set of unique changes happening in the world today, we now believe that it is imperative to *rethink the entire process and concepts of strategy formulation and deployment.* One of the most important changes is the emergence of a brand new type of competitor.

The Stealth Competitor: Supremacy In Jeopardy

A few years ago, the CEOs of the two dominant book retailers in the United States – Barnes & Noble and Borders – were sitting in their respective offices, listening to the business news on CNN's *Moneyline*, contemplating ways of taking away some of each other's business.

During the newscast, there was a short interview with a gentleman named Jeff Bezos, who announced that he had formed a company named *amazon.com*, which, effective immediately, would start selling books online through the Internet. Furthermore, he stated that amazon.com would carry over one million titles, a hundred times the average bookstore, that the price would be 30 to 50 percent less than in a bookstore, and that a purchase could be made in a couple of minutes from the comfort of one's home by simply using a PC.

A few weeks later, the CEO of Merrill Lynch was thinking about ways and means to compete with Smith Barney while watching the same TV program. Another young entrepreneur announced the launch of an online brokerage company called *E-Trade.com*, which would allow individuals to trade stocks from their home PCs at a fraction of the cost of trading through a broker.

. . . Ama . . . who? E . . . who? Price . . . who? Doing . . . what? must have been the reaction of these CEOs on the day of these announcements. All were caught completely off guard and since then, despite the dot-com crash, many of these new companies have become each CEO's biggest nightmare.

The day that amazon.com went online, Barnes & Noble's and Borders' business models were put in jeopardy. The day that E-Trade.com went online, Merrill Lynch's business model of selling stocks through thousands of highly commissioned salespeople was put in jeopardy.

Surprise! Surprise! Surprise!

Why were Ford, General Motors, and Chrysler caught by surprise and unable to see that smaller, high quality automobiles from Japan would drastically erode their market shares? After all, the Big Three were the dominant players in that game and had the resources to employ hundreds of futurists who could have foreseen just that.

Why was Singer, which had invented the sewing machine, and had put one in just about every home in the developed world, caught in the same trap? Why was IBM, the powerhouse of the computer industry, also taken by surprise by Apple's introduction of the first PC? Why was Wang, which invented the word processor, caught in a similar trap when

PCs emerged that could handle word processing as well as just about any computing task the business world would need?

Why were RCA and Zenith also caught completely off guard by Sony's introduction of a VCR linked to a TV set? After all, they were the largest, strongest, and richest in their industry and should have foreseen Sony's entrance into their sandbox.

Why were Polaroid and Kodak surprised by Sony's introduction of the Mavica digital camera in 1984, an event that has completely disrupted their business existence and to which neither company has found an adequate response more than twenty-five years later?

Two Important Questions

- Why is it that astute and intelligent CEOs, who have built successful companies, can be caught by surprise and find their business models in jeopardy overnight?

- What can be done to mitigate, or even reverse, this phenomenon?

Well established, dominant enterprises, or even an entire industry, can be "killed" or seriously injured by the advent of a so-called "stealth" competitor that had not been on the CEO's "radar screen."

Stuck In The Current Sandbox

In our view, many executives fail to anticipate the advent of stealth competitors that may put them out of business because they are stuck in the *current* competitive sandbox. In other words, their time is consumed with their preoccupation with *current* products, for *current* customers, in *current* market segments residing in *current* geographic markets. Although this is a necessary element of management, a more vital responsibility is to have a heightened concern about the company's *future* products, *future* customers, *future* markets, and *future* competitors. This should, in particular, include the stealth competitor that may come from *another sandbox* or from any of the other sources we will now explore.

Disruptive Changes Create Stealth Competitors

There are five broad areas from which a stealth competitor can emerge and become a CEO's worst nightmare.

- **Political/Regulatory Environment**

    These are radical changes that occur in either the political or the regulatory arenas. Some political examples are the breakup of the Soviet Union or the opening of China. These two changes will have an enormous impact on the future of businesses worldwide as they will bring another two billion people into a "free market" economy. On the other hand, they will also bring several thousand new competitors and a flood of commodities.

- **Demographics**

    Changes in demographics are another source that can disrupt many industries simultaneously. There are four types of demographics that can cause such disruption:

    - income distribution

    - age distribution

    - education levels

    - population shifts/mixes

An example is the aging of populations in Japan, the United States, and Europe, and the opposite trend in places like Mexico and Asia. This dichotomy will disrupt the strategies of many corporations. Oil companies, for instance, should be re-thinking their concept of the self-service gas station since older people are not as mobile and so cannot serve themselves as easily as younger drivers. Healthcare providers also need to be rethinking their approaches in these markets, since the health requirements of younger people are radically different from those of older patients.

If you are a manufacturer of exercise equipment, for example, the older people of the Western World will need radically different exercise machines than the "Young Turks" in other countries. If you want to achieve supremacy in your field, you will need a strategy that can accommodate this dichotomy – or a stealth competitor might be just around the corner.

Industry/Market Structural Changes

Radical changes in the structure of an industry or market will always bring disruption to many companies. In this category, one needs to monitor such elements as deregulation, which caused havoc in the airline industry in the 1980s and the energy industry in the 1990s; or privatization, such as is happening to many state-owned telecom and postal service organizations in several countries; or consolidation as is currently happening in the oil, drug, and several other industries; or the rationalization of industries. Each of these events will disrupt the strategies of many companies simultaneously.

Perception

This is one of the most difficult to detect, but it can disrupt companies in a significant way. It is the change in perception that customers have about a company's product. The ways in which customers perceive products are not static. Their perception of the look, feel, or benefits of the products they buy changes over time. An example is the cigarette. In the '50s and '60s smoking was "cool." In the '80s and '90s, it was "uncool." That change in perception will eventually bring that entire industry to its knees.

Another example is "fast food." For decades, McDonald's seemed invincible, with a business model that enabled it to expand quickly, maintain quality, and contain costs. Yet, partially because of a change in perception about the health concerns surrounding meat, cheese, and fried foods, Subway Sandwiches recently surpassed McDonald's with the most locations in the United States by offering a different menu with "healthier" options. Meanwhile, McDonald's supremacy has diminished in recent years.

Technology

Technological advances, obviously, can also bring disruption to almost any industry. Two kinds of technological advances can have this type of impact. One consists, naturally, of breakthroughs such as the laser, the microprocessor, the Internet, and the science of biotechnology.

Another is the convergence, or fusion, of different technologies, such as the marriage of computer and telecommunication technologies or the coupling of computers and biotechnology.

Changes Come In Three Sizes

Changes that may emanate from any of the above sources come in three sizes – micro, macro, and mega.

Micro changes are those that happen "once in a while" and are found at ground level. They are relatively easy to detect and we take care of these routinely, then go on with our lives. Micro changes have limited effects, impacting a very limited number of products, customers, or markets. An example might be the deregulation of the Italian post office. Although an important event in Italy, the effects of that change will probably be limited to Italy's borders.

Macro changes affect a much broader array of products, customers, or markets. They are "once in a generation" types of changes and can only be detected from around 20,000 feet above the Earth. Macro changes are not as easily detected as micro changes. Failure to detect a macro change could be fatal to your company. One such change is at work today and many CEOs have not noticed – the dichotomy in the age demographics of the Western World versus Mexico and Asia. This dichotomy will cause every company that does, or intends to do, business in these areas of the world, to rethink their product designs or service offerings.

If you are in the insurance business, for example, you will

need to develop a significantly different mix of insurance products for these diverging markets. If you want to achieve supremacy in your field, you will need a strategy that can accommodate this dichotomy or a stealth competitor may be waiting just around the corner.

Mega changes are "once in a century" type changes. They can usually be detected in their embryonic stage. But they are different enough in character that many executives don't quite understand them and, therefore, cannot assess the implications of these changes on their businesses. This can be fatal since mega changes affect *every product, every customer, every market, every company, every industry, in every country on the planet.* They will also affect the "genetic code" of every enterprise and usually are the source of dozens of "stealth" competitors. This is because their disruption is usually brought on by the advent of radical new technology. Two such technologies are currently giving many CEOs fits. One is the Internet, whose impact is, in fact, just beginning to become evident to many companies that had dismissed it after the dot-com debacle. The other is biotechnology, whose impact is yet to come, but will be much more far-reaching than the Internet.

Stealth competitors accompany these mega changes because it is usually an advanced guard of people who are first to understand these new technologies, and who use them before established companies recognize their value or are willing to roll the dice on their potential uses. Witness to this phenomenon is the advent of all the dot-coms during the '90s that were started by young people who understood the capabilities of the Internet and how to use these capabilities against well entrenched, but totally unprepared, companies.

Stealth Readiness Test

Here are some questions to ask yourself to determine your readiness vis-à-vis the appearance of a stealth competitor:

- Is your strategy ready for an unforeseen, unexpected stealth competitor that could become your worst nightmare?

- Have you anticipated what strategy a "stealth competitor" might conceive to establish supremacy in your sandbox?

- Do you know what "modus operandi" that competitor would use to deploy that strategy?

- Have you identified which company(ies) is a possible candidate(s) to become a stealth competitor(s)?

- Do you have a plan to respond to a stealth competitor?

- Have you explored being a stealth competitor in someone *else's* sandbox?

Disruptive Events Demand A Disruptive Strategy

Because these changes will alter the fundamental structures of these industries, our view is that CEOs will not only need to conceive strategies that change the rules of the game, but strategies that will also *change the nature of the game itself.* They will need to formulate strategies that are as "disruptive" to their competitors as the changes that are disrupting the structure of the industry in the first place. Only a strategy that disrupts the *status quo* will result in competitive supremacy for its creator. Such a strategy obliges competitors who want to play to do so by abiding by rules set by that same creator. This radical departure from traditional strategy concepts provides the pathway to competitive supremacy.

3

Supremacy Begins With a Clear Strategy for the Future, Not the Present

"People are surprised by the future because they have not been looking."

Assuming that you accept the concept of gaining supremacy over your competitors, you will probably then ask, "How do we do it?" The remainder of this book will answer that question.

Formulating the business strategy of the enterprise is the top item of every CEO's job description. As a result, one would think that every company would have a clearly articulated and explicit strategy. Our work with over four hundred corporations around the world has not proven that to be true. In fact, we find that companies fall into one of four categories that revolve around two key capabilities – the organization's operational prowess and its strategic prowess.

Strategic prowess is the kind of thinking that occurs in an organization that is *what* in nature. In other words, "*What* are we and *what* do we want to become?" Operational prowess is the kind of thinking that occurs in an organization that is *how* in nature or, "*How* do we get there?"

An element that adds to the difficulty of understanding the strategy of the business is that most people cannot distinguish between *strategy* and *operations*. Many have difficulty separating *strategy* and *strategic thinking* from *operations* and *operational thinking*. Although both types of thinking go on simultaneously in every organization, we have observed that these are practiced to different degrees of proficiency.

The difference can be explained by the following illustration.

In quadrant **A**, we find companies that have a well articulated strategy, well communicated and well understood by everyone in the organization. They know *what* they want to become. Furthermore, they are very competent operationally. They know *how* to get there.

An example of a company falling into this quadrant was IBM under the leadership of former CEO Lou Gerstner, with the formulation and deployment of his "co-centric computing" strategy. Other companies with clear strategies are Disney under Michael Eisner, Dell Computer under Michael Dell, Wal-Mart under Sam Walton and David Glass, Home Depot under Bernie Marcus and Arthur Blank, Sony under Akio Morita, Honda under Mr. Honda, and Microsoft under Bill Gates.

In quadrant **B**, we find companies that are operationally competent but strategically deficient. Many of the companies pursuing a me-too strategy fall into this quadrant.

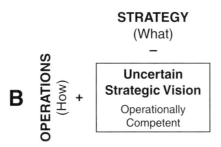

In quadrant **C**, we find companies that have a clear strategy. Their difficulty is making it happen operationally. A good example recently has been the PC industry with its dozens of competitors all trying to be the best "Wintel" clone they can be. Clear strategy, but unfortunately, most of them have been unable to execute well operationally and the winners and losers change almost every day.

In quadrant **D**, we find the worst of both worlds.

Unfortunately, the list of examples is not very long because if you find yourself in this quadrant, you are not around long enough to talk about it.

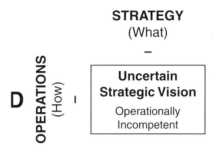

In which quadrant do you think most companies find themselves? We have asked this question to more than three thousand CEOs all over the world and the answer is always the same. Eighty to ninety percent of these CEOs tell us that most companies reside in quadrant **B**: operationally competent but strategically deficient. Many CEOs even include their own company in this observation. In other words, most executives can keep the "numbers" coming out right quarter after quarter, but they don't have a shared understanding of what the company will look like as a result of all that churning. We call this the "Christopher Columbus School of Management":

- When he left, he did not know where he was going.

- When he got there, he did not know where he was.

- When he got back, he could not tell where he had been.

A good strategy should work to the benefit of an organization over a long period of time, which implies that most companies should be in the **A** quadrant (+/+). Our experience has shown that most companies are actually in quadrant **B**, begging the question: "Why?" Our answer to this question is that most executives are so mired in operational issues that they seldom have time to do any "strategizing." They spend all their time fighting fires and don't have time to think strategically. Others may have what they believe to be a strategy, yet it is only an extrapolation of the past and only deals with the present without any consideration for future events and trends. This is how most "five-year plans" are constructed.

The best strategists are the ones whose organizations can achieve supremacy over long periods of time and are able to foresee potential disruptive trends, then create a "disruptive" strategy that will change the game in the *future*.

Key Skills

The creation of a "disruptive" strategy that will breed supremacy requires the mastery of two skills:

- Anticipation of future trends and their implications on society as well as on the organization

- Understanding of the organization's strategic capabilities that can be leveraged into these future trends

Yet, more and more CEOs we work with tell us that it is not possible to predict the future because changes are occurring faster and faster. As a result, they claim, no one can keep up – much less predict what else will happen in the future. To some extent, they are right.

Although this claim is partly true, the notion that change happens too quickly to be anticipated is somewhat of a myth. Our experience leads us to a different hypothesis. In our view, there are two modes to deal with changes: proactively or reactively. Many executives deal with most changes in a reactive mode. Their skill is *corrective* in nature rather than being proactive, or *anticipatory*. Proof of this is in the pudding. If their key skill was anticipatory, why were the CEOs and senior executives of thousands of corporations around the world caught by surprise by the advent of the Internet?

Envision The Future

"How can anyone anticipate what the future will look like? The future is a *big* place, and no one has a crystal ball." This is usually the reasoning we hear immediately after we offer the aforementioned hypothesis. But the *arena* in which a company will compete in the future is not one with a limitless number of variables.

In fact, this reaction has a very simple and rational explanation. It has been shown that many things that look big and complex at first glance turn out to be an assembly of a limited number of smaller elements when scrutinized more closely. This is, in reality, what the future arena in which a company will compete looks like. The Future Business Arena – or "sandbox" as we at DPI refer to it – in which any company finds itself consists of twelve discrete compartments from which disruptive trends might emerge:

- Economic/Monetary trends

- Political/Regulatory trends

- Social/Demographic trends

- Market conditions

- Customer attributes/habits

- Competitor profiles

- Next generation technology

- Manufacturing capabilities/processes

- Product design/content/features

- Sales/Marketing methods

- Distribution, delivery, and service methods

- Human/Natural/Financial resources

Once the complexity of the future business arena has been deciphered into these twelve "building blocks," one can begin to anticipate what the future will look like. By placing yourself and your key executives in a "time machine," moving yourself ahead "x" years, and describing the characteristics that each compartment will have at that time, you will have a very good "picture" of the future.

Then comes the next objection: "We don't have any futurists in our company. How can we foresee changes that will occur in the future? No one has a crystal ball." The good news is that you don't need a guru to predict the future. Our contention is that most changes that will impact your business ten years from now are in place today. *Most changes that will affect a company announce themselves well in advance of the time they will strike.*

Naturally, one cannot be a hundred percent right about the future, and totally unexpected events do occur, but if you're always looking ahead and have a dynamic process of strategy, you will be much better prepared to deal with these events, and deal with them proactively rather than being at their mercy.

As John Naisbitt, the renowned futurist, has said: "The best way to predict the future is to understand the present." In other words, the future has "folded" itself into the present, and one must "unfold" it to discover what is on the horizon. You must "go back" to the present to "see the future." But of course, if you have not been looking, you will always have a reactive, me-too strategy that will not bring supremacy.

By having an understanding of what the future sandbox will look like, you increase the probability of creating a strategy that breeds supremacy over your competitors and brings your shareholders greater value over time. And "supremacy" is not a dirty word!

4

Don't Change the Rules, Change the *Game*

"Change how customers buy, and how companies compete."

As mentioned in the *Preface*, "supremacy" is not an absolute numeric advantage over competitors, but rather the *degree of control* a company has over its competitors. The thesis proposed earlier in this book is that the ability to *control* the future "sandbox" that once depended on "changing the rules of play" now requires "changing the game itself."

There is a fine, but extremely important, nuance between the two concepts. The following examples are presented to illustrate that distinction.

Wal-Mart

Until Wal-Mart came on the scene, the department store game

and the rules for these retailers were the same for all the players across the country. The game was played this way:

- Stores were located in city centers and nearby suburban areas.

- The offering consisted of "dry," non-perishable goods.

- Marketing was "pull" oriented.

- Periodic sales on selected items occurred.

Wal-Mart first started by changing the rules. Contrary to the other chains that offered lower prices only on certain items each week, Sam Walton introduced the concept of "everyday low prices."

Not satisfied, Walton went even further and *changed the game itself* when he introduced several additional concepts. First, he avoided large cities and located his stores in mid-size, rural towns. Second, he clustered ten to twelve stores around a warehouse that could replenish these stores within twenty-four hours. Third, he stocked the shelves with both perishable and non-perishable goods. Fourth, he instituted a program to exert severe pressure on suppliers to continuously reduce their costs and prices to Wal-Mart.

The game had never been played in this manner. Sam Walton created a *new* game that put Wal-Mart on a path to strategic supremacy. To this day, some forty years later, K-Mart, Sears, and JC Penney are playing to Wal-Mart's rules and have yet to develop adequate counter-strategies. In fact, all have fallen into economic hard times as a result. In the meantime, the gap between Wal-Mart and its competitors gets wider and wider.

amazon.com

In book selling, the game was played in a well-known manner. In order to play the game, one built a chain of stores, stocked them with as many books as could be squeezed into each store's space, and then waited for people to come in, browse, and hopefully buy a book or two. Two chains – Borders and Barnes & Noble – attempted to change these rules by building stores several times larger than had been seen before, and carrying over 100,000 book selections compared to 10,000 in the traditional bookstore. Furthermore, they encouraged browsing the shelves by selling coffee and arranging comfortable reading areas. The new rules worked in their favor extremely well as they took more and more market share away from the operators of smaller stores.

These new rules, however, were still designed for the familiar game board of "bricks and mortar." Then along came the Internet, and amazon.com created a brand new game. Amazon shunned the traditional concept of company stores – bricks and mortar – and, instead, enabled the purchase of books right off the Internet, offering a selection of over a million titles at significant discounts. Furthermore, it allowed this to be done from home with the use of a PC. The order is confirmed while online and the book arrives at the buyer's door within twenty-four to thirty-six hours, all without the need to go anywhere near a bookstore. New game, no bricks and mortar, new game board – the Internet – and totally new rules set by amazon. To this day, Borders and Barnes & Noble have yet to come up with a counterstrategy while they watch amazon gradually establishing its supremacy over the industry.

CNN

The network TV industry was once dominated by three networks that understood the game they were in and played by its rules. The game was established and followed in robot-like lockstep: standard broadcast capability, variety programming with kids' programs in the morning, soaps, talk and game shows in the afternoon, a news hour at dinner time, sitcoms in the evening and sports on the weekend. The three networks – ABC, CBS, and NBC – understood the rules of this game so well that no one network ever gained supremacy over its two other rivals. In fact, none of the three had a distinctive strategy. They were all imitating each other, with the result that, each year, they played musical chairs as to which one would get 23, 22, or 21 market share.

Ted Turner entered the game, didn't like it, and decided to create a new game on a new game board. Instead of going standard broadcast, he used cable and satellite. Instead of variety programming, he opted for an all-news format. Instead of staying domestic, he went international. And which game has established its supremacy as the premier news organization in the world and produced more wealth for its shareholders in the last twenty years? The answer: CNN, the name Turner gave to his new game. Watch for new games to emerge from this arena as satellite, cable, and broadband technologies become more established worldwide.

Home Depot

For the last fifty years or so, if you were doing some repairs to your home and needed lumber or a few screws, you walked over to your neighborhood lumberyard and picked up a few two-by-fours, then made your way to the neighborhood hardware store to pick up the screws. Every community had its mom-and-pop lumberyard and hardware store, and the game was played that way across America...until Arthur Blank and Bernie Marcus arrived on the scene and decided to radically change the nature of the game.

Instead of the ten thousand square foot mom-and-pop store, Blank and Marcus built massive, one hundred thousand square foot monsters that stored both lumber and hardware in quantities and varieties unseen before. To appeal to the amateur handyman, they staffed each section with a craftsman licensed in that trade, which reassured the buyer that he was being served by a knowledgeable professional. Furthermore, they built hundreds of stores around the country so quickly that they established their supremacy over the mom-and-pop operators and other home centers that had popped up before any of them realized what had hit them. When was the last time you saw the names Channel, Pergament, or Builder's Square? The game was changed for good.

Roberts Express
(now called FedEx Custom Critical)

There was a time in the trucking industry when the rules were the same for all the players. The basic rules were:

- Buy a fleet of trucks.

- Determine whether to concentrate on short hauls or long hauls.

- Hunt down customers.

- Always try to get a return load from wherever you go to minimize empty legs.

- Beat down your competitors on price, which leads to razor thin margins and volatile periods of profit and losses.

When the industry was deregulated in the late '70s, most trucking companies saw that event as an opportunity to extend their routes into other companies' territories. However, they continued to play the game as they had before, which only led to more intense competition and even greater amounts of red ink.

The management of one company, Roberts Express, looked at the same event and saw an opportunity to change the game itself. Let's say that you run an auto assembly plant in Detroit, and you are on a JIT basis with your suppliers. Engines, for example, are delivered one shift prior to the time they are used. One day, your engine supplier has problems of his own and the engines don't show up. You are now faced with the possibility of having to temporarily shut down the plant and send five thousand employees home.

This is when Roberts Express's strategy kicks in. Roberts has a network of two thousand independent truck owners who identify themselves under the company's brand name. These truck owners are located across the country waiting for your call. While you are on the phone with the Roberts dispatcher, he or she is locating, through the Roberts proprietary satellite system, the truck nearest to your engine supplier's plant. Within seconds you have a guarantee that the engines will be picked up within plus or minus fifteen minutes of a specific hour and delivered to your plant within the same window, also at a specific hour. This is a radically different game.

On top of this, Roberts has built-in cost and flexibility advantages. Roberts doesn't own any of the trucks, thus saving a large capital expenditure that weighs down other trucking companies. The drivers, who buy their own trucks, are all independent contractors, which means that Roberts has none of the administrative responsibilities that come with carrying those employees. But the beauty of the strategy is that Roberts gets premium prices in an industry that is renowned for cutthroat pricing.

In fact, Roberts's strategy resulted in such a large "supremacy gap" over the rest of the industry that its success attracted the eye of another company that believes in strategic supremacy: FedEx. It is now a member of the FedEx family.

Southwest Airlines

Since deregulation in the early '70s, the airline industry and all its players have played the game in the same manner. All have a "hub and spoke" system; all use aircraft of different sizes and configurations manufactured by different companies; all have invested billions of dollars in sophisticated reservation systems; and all continuously complain about how stupid an industry they are in with stupid competitors and even stupid customers.

All . . . that is, except Southwest Airlines, which has made a profit every day since its inception in 1972. Why? Southwest has created its own game! Instead of operating through hubs, it operates on a point-to-point basis. It floods these two locations with up to a dozen flights per day at "everyday low – and only one – price," thus drawing a multitude of first-time passengers who would normally travel by bus. Instead of using multiple aircraft, it employs a single aircraft – the Boeing 737 – and, as far as a sophisticated, costly reservation system . . . it has none!

Whose strategy is quickly ascending towards supremacy over the industry? You're right. Southwest. The strategy is so far superior to those of the other airlines that Boeing custom built a "stretch" version of its 737 model for Southwest only. Furthermore, all of Southwest's growth has been organic, whereas most other airlines' growth has been through acquisitions. For thirty years now, none of the other airlines have been able to put together a viable response to this strategy and Southwest has grown year after year at their expense.

The University of Phoenix

The cozy world of university presidents, deans, and professors is about to be dismantled in the next ten to fifteen years. The game in this industry is well known to all the players and has been in place for several hundred years. These rules are simple to understand:

- Choose a charming geographic location.

- Build a lot of buildings, each to accommodate a different discipline.

- Give these buildings a distinctive architectural look and feel.

- Hire "name" professors who will put the university "on the map."

- Promise these professors "tenure," or lifetime employment, if they enhance their reputations by getting their works published.

- Seek wealthy alumni to contribute to your endowment.

- Start an MBA summer school to attract high level executives to solidify your relationships with industry.

That formula has worked successfully for many universities for several centuries. Lurking in the shadows is a stealth competitor that is not on most traditional universities' "radar screens." This new entrant is called the University of Phoenix. Unlike the traditional universities, the U of P does not have a campus in a charming little town. In fact, it has no campus at all. Nor does it have any buildings – no bricks and mortar. Therefore, no classrooms. And even more interesting – there are no students and no professors on site. What the University of Phoenix does have, however, is the Internet . . . and ninety thousand students, very few of whom are in Phoenix. It also is a public shareholder company with a market cap of over $2 billion. The University of Phoenix's forecast calls for an enrollment of over a hundred thousand online students and annual revenues of $1 billion in the next three years.

John Sperling, the university's founder and a former history professor, has not only changed the rules, but has *changed the game* of higher education itself.

Dell Computer

Michael Dell is another individual who has built a powerhouse, multi-billion dollar company in a few short years by first changing the rules and then by changing the game itself. Instead of marketing computers through retail stores, as the industry rules dictated up to that point, he decided to market PCs through direct response marketing methods. This was an attempt to change the rules, which enjoyed early success. But the company's products were the same as those of its competitors. A few years after the company's creation, Dell decided to change the game itself. He married the concept of direct marketing with that of on-demand, made-to-order computers.

The result? A multi-billion dollar company that has the highest revenue per employee, the lowest inventory per employee, the highest return on capital, and a stock price that has outperformed the market by a factor of a large scale earthquake, despite the volatility of the PC market.

In 1997, Dell decided to change the game again by changing its direct marketing method from catalogs to the Internet. Only a few months after it extended this mechanism around the world, Dell was booking over $10 million in orders per day. Dell has caused other computer companies, such as Compaq, to rethink their own strategies and try to do things Dell's way. Unfortunately, they found themselves on Dell's game board, whose rules are controlled by Dell. Most of its competitors have recognized the supremacy of Dell's strategy and have since given up.

Starting from zero, Dell was a $30 billion company by 2002. Overall, Michael Dell's strategy is relatively simple: commoditization of differentiated products. Dell likes to take innovative products, such as PCs, and turn them into commodities that can be assembled quickly from pre-stocked components and tailored to each customer's separate needs. Since the entire PC market has been commoditized, Dell is the sole player with a market advantage. This strategy *anticipated* this condition years ago and *planned* for it. With 14 percent of the global PC market, Dell could be considered to have achieved "supremacy" already, but its strategic intent says that supremacy will come when the company has *40 percent* of the worldwide *computer* market – not only the PC market. His strategy is being extended to include servers, switches, modems, storage, and any other piece of hardware that is related to PCs for both the business and *home* markets. And *supremacy*, not adequacy, is the goal. Watch out IBM, Cisco, Gateway, and anyone else in computer retail – your sandbox is about to be disrupted in a major way.

Boeing's Strategic Coup

For most of the twentieth century, Boeing had established its supremacy in the aircraft design and construction sandbox. Its supremacy was so pronounced that almost all other competitors gave up and Boeing had the sandbox pretty much to itself.

That was so until a consortium of European governments decided, as an attempt to blunt Boeing's supremacy, to form a company to build commercial aircraft, which they named "Airbus." Airbus's strategy was very simple: "Copycat Boeing." In other words, whatever size aircraft Boeing made, Airbus decided to duplicate it. And because Boeing was not accustomed to intense competition, Airbus eventually took 40 percent of the market away from Boeing.

For a while, Boeing did not know how to respond and it engaged in a battle with Airbus whereby each company attempted to outdo the other by making bigger and bigger planes. Both companies were pursuing an "imitation" strategy, basically cloning each other. For Boeing, this was not a winning proposition. Boeing had to rethink its strategy. Finally, at the Bourget Air Show in 1999, Boeing went public with its new strategy and announced that it would build a "mega" jetliner that would carry over eight hundred people. It would do this by "stretching" its 747 model rather than build a brand new aircraft.

A "mega" plane had been part of Airbus's thinking as well. But Airbus had been reluctant to pursue such a gigantic aircraft because of its enormous development costs. However, in light of Boeing's announcement, Airbus had no other choice now than to aggressively explore this path. In an attempt to try to finally separate and differentiate from Boeing's shadow, Airbus announced that its mega plane would not be an extension of a current model but, instead, would be a brand new design. In March of 2000, Airbus introduced this new model with great fanfare. In an attempt to outdo Boeing, Airbus designed an aircraft that would be a "double-decker," like the buses in London. Airbus received press from around the world and many pundits started predicting the end of Boeing's supremacy and possibly the beginning of the end of Boeing.

Exactly two weeks later, Boeing held its own press conference and no one expected to hear what they heard. Boeing announced to the world that, instead of imitating Airbus, Boeing was going to *reinvent the game.* The company told the world's press that it had decided to scrap its plans to extend the 747. Instead, it would build a new mid-size, *supersonic aircraft* that would reduce travel time by 40 percent, with the same operating costs as the jet-propelled airplane. All the experts agreed immediately. This was a much better strategy than Airbus's, since everyone knows that frequent fliers are not interested in traveling with *more people,* they simply want to get there *more quickly.*

Boeing has decided to change the game in an attempt to regain its supremacy. Now, for the key question: Do you really think that Boeing ever intended to build a "stretched" 747? My answer is: "Never in a million years!"

That announcement made back in 1999 was, in my view, simply a ploy to entice Airbus into action and commit itself to a strategy that Boeing knew they could make obsolete very quickly. Airbus is now in the difficult position of having to retract its "mega plane" strategy and switch to a supersonic platform, about which they have very little knowledge, putting them three to four years behind Boeing.

One of the other concepts that we have been promoting for over twenty years is that a good strategy allows you to manage your competitor's strategy to your advantage as well as your own. However, this can only be achieved by attaining *supremacy of thinking,* which then leads to *supremacy of strategy.*

The Chemical Industry

The chemical industry has approximately two hundred companies in its sandbox. In a study done recently by the *Chemical Market Reporter,* it was discovered that only ten companies exceeded the S&P 500 in shareholder value growth since 1996. The two top performing companies,

Valspar and Cambrex, achieved this level of supremacy by *"fundamentally changing the industry structure itself."*

While most companies in this sector are under-performing the S&P 500, Valspar revenues and earnings have grown at better than 13 percent annually for the last twenty years. Cambrex's shareholder value increased by 900 percent more than the S&P 500. Both did it by changing the game.

Valspar looked at its competitors and saw big companies with strong global brands supported by huge advertising and marketing budgets – companies entrenched with retail chains across the world that enabled them to control the shelf space in stores – and substantial economies of scale on the manufacturing side. Valspar created its own game. It decided to ignore the traditional retail channels and chose to focus exclusively on the upcoming "big box" retailers such as Home Depot, Lowe's, and Sam's Club. Valspar then decided not to invest in developing its own brand and did only "private label" products for these retailers. And last, but not least, it decided to buy, on a need-to basis, ailing manufacturing plants rather than build new ones. All these changes gave Valspar considerable cost advantages for which their competitors have not yet found a response. In the meantime, Valspar reigns supreme and the company has increased shareholder value by a sum larger than its closest six competitors.

Cambrex, competing in a different part of the sandbox, changed the game in a different manner. It decided on a strategy dependent on technological innovation. It uses its technological prowess to help its customers develop "new-to-the-world" products that don't exist anywhere. As a result, Cambrex has seen, and is planning to continue, double-digit growth.

Charles Schwab: Strategist "Par Excellence"

Some individuals have such an innate understanding of the concept of attaining strategic supremacy by changing the game rather than just the rules, that they have done it several times. Charles Schwab is such an individual. Schwab has an uncanny ability to anticipate future trends before his competitors do, and then create a new game.

Schwab founded Charles Schwab & Company in the 1970s by first changing the rules of the stock brokerage business, starting with the most cherished rule in the industry: He set transaction fees at half the industry norm. Furthermore, unlike his competitors, Schwab offered no research, one of the most costly services a broker extends. With these rule changes, Schwab spawned the discount brokerage business. Unfortunately, many imitators sprang up.

In 1995, however, Schwab decided to change the game itself. Schwab saw the growing dissatisfaction with ever increasing, and sometimes exorbitant, management fees that mutual funds imposed on their investors. The company introduced a program named One Source, which permitted investors to purchase a mix of mutual funds from a single source – Charles Schwab, naturally – rather than do so from each mutual fund company individually. The One Source program allowed each investor to choose from a portfolio of over seven hundred funds without paying any commission whatsoever, and to switch from one fund to another without any penalty charge. The concept completely revolutionized the marketing of mutual funds and found the industry leader, Fidelity, asleep at the switch.

In 1997, Schwab decided to create yet another game. He introduced a program that allowed investors to trade stocks online. Within a matter of weeks, Schwab was trading over $4 billion per week, which represented over 50 percent of its revenues. It has since climbed to over 90 percent of its revenues. This time, Schwab caught Merrill Lynch asleep at the switch. Until Schwab introduced this program, stocks were traded over the phone through an army of highly paid sales people backed by expensive research. This new game has put that model in jeopardy and has forced all the brokerage houses to rethink their strategies and explore how they might respond. Unfortunately for them, the existing rule of selling through highly paid sales people makes it extremely difficult to change but, more importantly, they would be playing on Schwab's game board and according to Schwab's rules.

Still not satisfied, Schwab has decided to change the game yet again. In June 2000, the company announced the purchase of U.S. Trust Corp., a money manager and financial adviser to the carriage trade where customers are not considered customers until they have been so for generations – not days, weeks, or months. What is Schwab doing in such an environment? Charles Schwab, being a very astute strategist, has glanced into the future and detected that there is a significant shift happening in the demographics of the United States. It is a fact that sometime between the years 2010 and 2015, 50 percent of the U.S. population will be over 55 years of age. Many of them will have inherited large sums of money and will be faced with complex issues in an attempt to manage this wealth and preserve it for their children. Over $13 trillion will be transferred from one generation to the next during this period. Many of the recipients of this wealth are probably current Schwab customers. Most will require personalized advice to help them optimize their returns. Do you get the connection? Is Charles Schwab about to create another new game?

On May 16, 2002 Charles Schwab changed the game *again*. In the past decade or so, there has emerged an army of so-called "financial planning consultants" who advise individuals on how to manage and invest their money. Thousands of independent, one-man shops have sprung up all over the country, many of which have questionable, if any, credentials. Putting up a shingle and claiming to be a financial planner is their only qualification to enter this thriving industry. Many people, including myself, have been reluctant to use their services because of their lack of known qualifications.

Enter Charles Schwab with a totally new game. Schwab has announced the creation of a "network of independent financial planners *certified* by Charles Schwab & Company." Independent financial planners will be invited to apply to become members of this network. But only those that pass a series of rigorous standards and abide by a stringent code of ethics will be accepted.

The Schwab reputation will be the backbone of the network and is bound to increase the credibility of those that can claim to have the Charles Schwab seal of approval. Obviously, these members will be expected to conduct their transactions through Schwab.

What new game will he invent next? Stay tuned!

Insurance By The Minute

From a zero-based start in the 1970s, Progressive Insurance has become the nation's fourth largest auto insurer with revenues of over $6 billion. It did so initially by changing the rules of play.

In the car insurance industry, there is a "golden" rule. "Don't insure drivers who are prone to accidents." That is an industry rule that no insurance company violates. That is, until Progressive entered the game and changed the rules. Progressive did the exact opposite and *only* insured individuals who had had accidents . . . and at a premium nonetheless.

Until Progressive came along, all insurers calculated their risk exposure with a particular driver based on that driver's age and an accident-free past. In other words, only insure those individuals who have not had an accident. As a result, one can calculate the probability of risk quite accurately. The difficulty with this approach is that every other insurer is doing the same and everybody ends up with a "me-too" strategy that might match, but never gain supremacy over, those competitors.

Progressive's strategy was designed to do the exact opposite. Somewhere along the way, Progressive noticed that people who have had one accident are less likely to have any more. Progressive's statisticians got to work and confirmed that the probability of someone having a second accident was *lower* than that of having their first. Thus, witness the continuing growth of Progressive to this day.

Now Progressive may be about to change the game itself.

Anticipating a future in which most people will be at ease with all the gadgets of the digital age, Progressive has conducted a pilot program in Texas that could revolutionize the auto insurance industry and make Progressive the focal point of that new game. In several cars, the company installed devices that measure the amount of time that the car is in use, who is driving and, through a link-up to a Global Positioning Satellite (GPS), where the car has been driven. All this data is captured online and transmitted back to Progressive, which then uses it to calculate that driver's premium. In other words, *insurance by the mile!* Like a meter in a parking lot, you only pay for the time used. Sounds like Progressive may have another home run on its hands, especially since giant competitor Allstate complains that such an approach "would require a massive restructuring of a well-functioning underwriting system."

FedEx: David Changes The Game On Goliath

There was a time not so long ago that all letters and small packages were delivered exclusively by the U.S. Postal Service, most of them within twenty-four hours. In the 1970s, however, the Postal Service began to renege on that promise with mail delivery taking as long as one week. This was not ideal performance for documents that needed urgent attention. Luckily, the game was about to be changed.

Fred Smith, who had no prior knowledge of how the Postal Service operated except to know that its performance was inadequate, was searching for a topic for a paper he was submitting in order to graduate from business school. His thesis proposed the formation of a company with a fleet of aircraft that would fly, point to point, between major cities and a central hub in Memphis – at night! During the day, an army of small trucks would meet the planes early each morning, collect the previous day's parcels originating from all over the country, and deliver them to recipients in that city "positively, absolutely by 10:30" that morning. In the afternoons, the same trucks would collect parcels from various customers and bring them to the planes waiting to fly them to Memphis for sorting, and then dispatch them to their respective destinations.

This was a radically different concept from the way the Postal Service played the game. In fact, Smith created a *brand new game.* A group of investors thought Smith's concept would be so disruptive for the Postal Service that they gave him $60 million in seed capital to get his company up and running.

For years, FedEx mocked and capitalized on the Postal Service's deficiencies and a full-scale war between the two emerged, which continued for over twenty-five years. Finally, in January 2001, the mighty U.S. Postal Service capitulated. In a rare and public admission of the supremacy of FedEx's strategy, the Postal Service decided to play the game according to the rules set by FedEx. It gave FedEx the largest contract it had ever awarded. The contract calls for FedEx to handle a large portion of the Postal Service's operations. Adding salt to the wound, the "treaty" also gives FedEx the right to place its own pick-up bins in every Post Office in the United States. This could be the first step towards the eventual takeover of the Post Office by FedEx.

The graduation paper? Smith's professor gave it a D minus! Genius is not often quickly recognized – giving strategic innovators the advantage of long lead times until their competitors gradually figure out the new game being played.

Strategic Quiz

What score would your "professor" give your current strategy? In order to assess the degree of supremacy you have over your competitors, or that they have over you, you may wish to answer the following questions:

Does your strategy . . .

1. correct past errors?	❑	1
2. address current conditions?	❑	2
3. exploit future trends?	❑	3

Is your strategy . . .

1. decreasing the gap between you and your competitors?	❑	1

2. keeping the gap the same?   ❏   2
3. increasing the gap?   ❏   3

Does your strategy allow you to . . .
   1. control the terms of play in your
       sandbox?   ❏   1
   2. manage your competitor's strategy
       as well as your own?   ❏   2
   3. grow at your competitors' expense?   ❏   3

Does your strategy . . .
   1. put you on a par with your
       competitors?   ❏   1
   2. give you a slight edge over your
       competitors?   ❏   2
   3. give you a significant advantage
       over your competitors?   ❏   3
   4. dominate your competitors?   ❏   4
   5. make competitors irrelevant?   ❏   5
   6. eliminate competitors?   ❏   6

Total:_____

Score Interpretation

If you scored 13 or more, you already reign supreme in your sandbox. You can stop reading at this point, unless of course, you want to learn why you are doing so well. On the other hand, if you scored between 10 and 13, you are doing reasonably well but the concepts in the remainder of this book will probably help take your organization to the "next and ultimate" level of strategy.

If you scored between 6 and 9, you are good but not yet in the "major league" of strategic concepts and processes. A well-developed strategy creation and deployment process could turbo-charge your company into the next strata or above. If you scored below 6, your current strategy is not working and it's time for a major rethink.

Disrupting The Future

The CEOs of three of the companies described in this chapter (Schwab, Progressive, and FedEx) obviously are excellent strategists and have an uncanny ability to disrupt their competitors' futures over and over again. This makes one wonder why so many executives often have difficulty fore-seeing trends or events that might seriously disrupt a healthy strategy and put it in jeopardy overnight. Our view is that most corporations lack a fundamental *process* of strategy. This is why, more than twenty years ago, we set about creating one. We call it *Strategic Thinking.*

5

Strategic Thinking: The Essence of Attaining Competitive Supremacy

"One must have supremacy of thinking before achieving supremacy of strategy."

As noted earlier, the majority of CEOs we surveyed placed their companies in the Christopher Columbus School of Management – that is, in the quadrant characterized by operational competence but strategic uncertainty. Intrigued, we started looking into the barriers, obstacles, and impediments that prevent companies from operating in the upper left quadrant, the ideal one to be in. To identify the various obstacles, we went back to these companies to find out what people who work in these organizations do.

Obstacles To Strategic Thinking

The first observation we made very quickly was that people who run companies spend a lot of their time in meetings of one kind or another. My friends at 3M, for example, tell me that when people are appointed "managers," they spend 80 to 90 percent of their time in meetings, talking and talking to one another! In many companies, these people have been meeting and talking for years.

The Strategy Suffers From "Fuzzy Vision"

It would seem logical, then, for people in management to have a shared and clear vision of what lies ahead for their organizations. However, when we asked each of them to describe what their company might look like in the future, we got very different pictures. Each person gave us a different version of what that "look" would be.

**Obstacles To
Good Strategic Thinking**

Strategies can suffer from fuzzy vision.

Management Is Engulfed In Operational Minutiae

That led us to our next question: "What do they talk about?" And what do you think we heard them talking about during all those meetings? Right! They talked about operational issues, rather than strategic issues. This means that the "look" of the organization starts being shaped by outside forces.

Operational

Strategic

Operational minutiae block strategic thought.

And there are many outside forces that will gladly take over the strategy and direction of your company if you abdicate your right to do so yourself. These forces include your customers by the nature of demands they make on your organization – those that you respond to and those to which you do not.

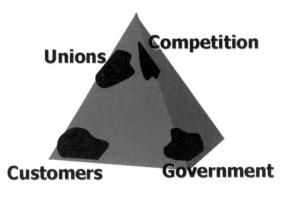

Corporate Profile is shaped by outside forces.

No Crisis, No Strategy

We further observed that when times are good, and all the charts, graphs, and numbers are going through the roof, executives have things on their minds other than asking themselves: "Where is this business going?"

Good times put off strategic thinking.

Only in times of crisis, when resources become scarce and limited resources must be allocated more carefully, does the need to think strategically surface. Our view is that strategic thinking is an ongoing process during good times or bad times. In fact, if you wait until the bad times, it obviously becomes more difficult to do.

No Formal Process

The most important obstacle to sound strategic thinking that we discovered was the lack of a *formal process.*

Strategy depends on a formal process.

Periodically, we would come across a well-intentioned management team that said to itself: "Let's go up to the mountaintop for a weekend and discuss where this business is going." People would then make their way to the retreat, sit around a table, put their elbows up, and start looking at each other. After seven minutes of silence, one of them would finally ask: "Now that we're here, what do we do? Where do we start?" After another seven minutes of silence, guess what kinds of issues they were discussing again. Right! Operational issues – the very issues they didn't want to discuss in the first place.

Even well-led and well-managed companies – including such clients as Caterpillar, 3M, Bekaert – did not have a formal process to help them decide what they wanted to become in the future. This observation led DPI to concentrate its efforts and research on the answer to a simple question: "If there is a process to help a company determine its future, what is that process?" In other words, "What questions should people be asking themselves while they are sitting around this table? And in what order should they go through these questions in order to create a strategy that could breed supremacy over their competitors?"

Therefore, when we work with a client, we bring the *questions* and we guide the management team through these questions in a structured and systematic manner. Again, however, it is *their input* going into the process and it is *their output* coming out of the process. This gives the management team complete and absolute ownership of the strategy. A strategy that has been created by the people who have a vital stake in the future of an organization gets implemented much more quickly and much more successfully than one that is imposed on the organization by an outside third party.

The Origins Of Strategic Thinking

The 1970s saw the advent of strategic planning as a key tool proposed by consultants to aid corporate managements in determining the future of their organizations. Most strategic planning systems, however, relied on historical data – numbers – that were generated internally. These systems required long and exhaustive analyses with a heavy numerical base. The result was an extrapolation of history into the future. The skill required: *quantitative analysis.*

Strategic Thinking, on the other hand, incorporates an assessment of both the internal and external environments.

The data are highly subjective and consist of the personal perceptions of each member of the management team. Most of the data are stored in each person's head. The key is to tap into that knowledge base and bring these perceptions into an objective forum for rational debate. The process involves a qualitative evaluation of the business and its environment and is both introspective and extrospective. *Strategic Thinking* is the ability to *synthesize* highly *qualitative* data into a rational strategy. The skill required: *qualitative synthesis.*

During the 1970s, when strategic planning was at its pinnacle, an avalanche of books appeared under a variety of titles: *Strategic Management, Corporate Strategy, Strategy THIS,* and *Strategy THAT.* Because of my experience in marketing positions at the time, I was attracted to many of these books and started browsing through them to gain a better understanding of strategy.

As I started going through these books, I made two very quick discoveries. First, every author who mentioned "strategy" assigned the word a different meaning. One author claimed that strategy was the *goal* and that operations was the *tactic.* The next author insisted that the "goal" definition was wrong. Rather, the goal was the *objective* and strategy was the *means.* The next author defined strategy as *long-term planning* and tactics as *short-term planning.* Needless to say, I became increasingly confused the more books I read.

The second discovery I made was that all these books were written by business school professors who ensconced themselves in business school libraries before posing the question of the century: "What has made General Electric so successful?" And without ever speaking to anyone at GE, but strictly by observing organizations from the outside, they concocted the "miracle" recipes that GE and these so-called winning organizations had used and then published books extolling their "findings."

At DPI, we decided to do our research in a very different manner. We said to ourselves: "Let's go and talk to real people who run *real* organizations and ask them how they go about deciding the future of their companies." And we did just that. We started interviewing CEOs in a variety of different size companies, in a variety of different industries, in dozens of countries. Eventually, we even sat in on meetings that CEOs had with their management teams while they were talking "strategy." Therefore, the concepts described in the remainder of this book are not "miracle" recipes pulled out of the sky. Rather, they represent a process that was extracted from the heads of real CEOs running real companies.

Supremacy: Taking Strategic Thinking To The Next Level

The *Strategic Thinking Supremacy* concepts we are describing in this book have their roots in our original process of *Strategic Thinking* that we developed and have perfected and validated over the last twenty-five years. However, our new *Strategic Thinking Supremacy Process* takes our original concepts to a higher level with the addition of new concepts, such as the description of the Future Business Area, the advent of "stealth" competitors, and the development of a Supremacy Model. Like our current process, however, our new *Strategic Thinking Supremacy Process* still starts with the CEO's vision for the future of the organization.

The CEO's Vision: The Cornerstone Of Strategy

As we began talking to CEOs, we noticed that within minutes of beginning each discussion, they would start speaking of a certain "vision" they had for the future of their company.

A CEO's Vision

Frequently what a CEO envisioned his or her company to "look like" in the future was somewhat different from what it "looks like" today.

What Is Strategic Thinking?

Creating a vision is akin to painting a picture. Warren Buffett, the renowned investor and founder of Berkshire Hathaway, describes it this way: "Berkshire is my painting, so it should look the way I want it to look."

In complete agreement with the above, we came to describe Strategic **Thinking**, as opposed to strategic planning, as the kind of thinking that goes on in the heads of the CEO and the management team as they attempt to transform their vision into a *profile*, or *picture*, of what the company will "look like" at some point in the future.

The Strategic Profile actualizes the vision.

They then would "hang" that profile, or picture, up as a target for all their plans and decisions. Decisions that fit inside the "frame" of the profile were pursued, while those that did not were abandoned. In other words, that profile, or picture, became the "filter" for all their plans and decisions.

How does a company's profile, the result of its
strategy, reflect itself in physical terms?

Target for all plans

Why would a CEO want to design a profile for the future of
the company? The answer is simple: to ensure that people
make consistent and intelligent decisions on behalf of the
company. Which leads to the next question: "If I want my
people to make good decisions on my behalf, what do I paint
inside that picture to help them do that?" or, "How does the
profile of a company transform itself into tangible or physical elements?" Or still, "What elements of a company could I
touch or feel that would be tangible evidence of its strategy
and direction?"

Inputs And Outputs

To this question, there are several answers. I could look
at the company's portfolio of current and announced
products. That would be one "clue." I could look at its
facilities to see what they produced and where they were
located. That would be another clue. I could look at its
base of customers and where they reside – its geographic

markets. I could examine its competitors and its suppliers. These are other clues. Gradually, as I look at each "piece" of the company, the "puzzle" starts taking shape in my mind as to what that organization will "look like" in the future.

- Products

- Facilities

- Technology

- Talent

- Customers

- Suppliers

- Industry segments

- Distribution methods

- Geographic markets

- Production capabilities

- Competitors

- Selling methods

The "look," or profile, of a company that is the "result" of its strategy resides in four of the areas listed above. Specifically, the profile of a company finds itself in the nature of:

- The products that the company decides to offer

- The customers to whom it offers these products

- The industry segments that it decides to pursue

- The geographic markets that it seeks

All the other elements listed above are either *inputs* to this profile or *outputs* from this profile.

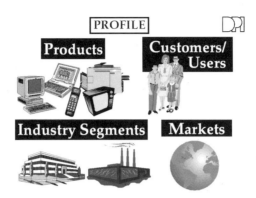

Key areas of the strategic profile

In order to give *clear* direction, however, the CEO must articulate and design a strategic profile that needs to have the following content:

- It needs to identify the nature of products that will be offered but, more importantly, the nature of products that will *not* be offered.

- It needs to identify the types of customers to concentrate on but, more importantly, the types of customers *not* to concentrate on.

- It needs to identify the industry segments to pursue but, more importantly, the industry segments *not* to pursue.

- It needs to identify the geographic markets to be sought but, more importantly, the geographic markets *not* to be sought.

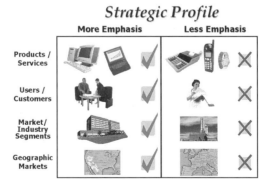

Strategic Profile includes areas of greater and lesser emphasis.

The Strategic Profile Becomes
A Filter For Decision Making

Why should a CEO's vision be transformed into a strategic profile of products, customers, industry segments, and geographic markets to emphasize more and, conversely, those to emphasize less? The answer is simple: to create a filter that will help employees make *consistent* and *logical* decisions on behalf of the company. And there are two types of decisions that will shape the "look" of the company over time.

The first is how resources are allocated. Most companies allocate resources through a budget mechanism. The difficulty with most budget systems is that they start at the lowest levels in the organization and creep their way up different silos. How the people at the lowest levels go about determining what they will accomplish in the next two or three years is by looking back at what *they have achieved in the last two to three years* – the numbers – and then projecting the numbers into the future while making minor adjustments for costs, inflation, and currency swings. This type of planning seeks to go forward by looking in the rearview mirror. It does nothing to change the "look" of the company. Basically, it takes the company in its current state and extrapolates that state into the future, yet does not advance the company's future ability to enhance its supremacy over its competitors.

Laurie Dippenaar, CEO of FirstRand in South Africa, describes his management team's use of the Strategic Filter created with our process in this manner:

> "One of the most valuable contributions to our thinking from the DPI process is that it provides a filter for the opportunities that you're swamped with. You can easily choose the ones that fit your strategy so you don't go chasing hares across the plains."

Which brings us to the next question: "How does management go about deciding on the line of demarcation between the items that should receive more emphasis and those that should receive less?" The answer to this important question lies in the fundamental concept of competitive supremacy: the *Driving Force*, which we will explore in the next chapter.

Strategic Thinking: Perspectives From The CEO's Chair

From time to time, we interview our CEO clients to gain insight into their perceptions of *Strategic Thinking* – how they use it and why. Here are excerpts from interviews with Rafaël Decaluwé, CEO of Belgium-based N.V. Bekaert, S.A., and three successive CEOs of Caterpillar, the earth moving equipment giant. Other full-length interviews appear later in this book.

Bekaert: Rewiring a Global Strategy

N.V. Bekaert, S.A. manufactures and supplies the steel cord found in just about every radial tire in the world. When Rafaël Decaluwé first became CEO in 1997 he had this to say about the role of *Strategic Thinking:*

> "After interviewing and debating with a number of people, not the least of which were the people on the board – who look at my rating sheet and my pay every year – I came to the conclusion that my primary task is shaping the vision of the company, communicating it, and getting it implemented. Now those are three things that are easily said, but not so easily done."

His perception at the time was that the company was strong operationally, yet needed a vision of the future to drive and grow its performance in the future. He looked at "solution-driven" consultants whom, he believed, would run the risk of not understanding the business, jumping to conclusions and, most importantly, achieving low credibility with management. He settled on a different approach – in the form of the DPI *Strategic Thinking Process.*

> "What I wanted was a methodology that involved the thinking of our own people. I would hope that the people who were working in this business for twenty and more years would have a better view and understanding of what this business

is capable of doing and where it should go, than an outside consultant who comes for three to six months, reviews and interviews your people, and then comes up with a so-called magic solution of what you should do for the next 'x' years.

"I was a firm believer after my previous experiences that a team comes up with better answers than an individual, and, therefore, if you can involve a team in that sort of thinking about strategy, your commitment of the group having contributed to it will be far larger and will make the implementation easier. I would certainly stand by that. So it starts from the philosophy of a CEO. In my own view, you must feel that, yes, you are CEO, but you also realize that as one individual, given the size of the company, you're in no way physically capable of managing and directing strategy and all the operational issues yourself. So I recognize my own limitations from a physical and intellectual point of view as my starting point on building an organization with a team. In that context, I have found the *Strategic Thinking* approach extremely helpful.

"If you ask me now what were the advantages of the *Strategic Thinking Process*, I was really looking for something that would force our people to think and come up with some answers. It did bring us much closer and the team definitely functioned much better. It gave us consensus. It led us to focus on a few critical issues. We started out with a long list and got it down to five. It led the whole group to take on ownership. And on top of that, it is applicable to any level. Not only can you do it for the group, you can do it for business units.

"I call it a 'do-it-yourself kit' for managers in terms of coming to think about where you are with your business and taking hold of it."

Caterpillar: Cat Lands on Its Feet

A company that DPI has had a relationship with since 1986 is Caterpillar, the world's leading manufacturer of heavy machines. We have worked with Caterpillar, using *Strategic*

Thinking, over the span of three successive CEOs. Although the company had been extremely successful for over eighty years, in the mid-1980s it found itself reeling from a thirty-year assault by Komatsu. And Caterpillar's top executives were at a loss about what to do next. Here's how each of three Caterpillar CEOs view their experience with DPI's *Strategic Thinking Process.*

George Schaefer, CEO, Caterpillar, Inc.
1985 – 1990

"We were floundering despite help from the top consultants available. We had too much good advice. We knew, soon after involving DPI, that we were moving in a more orderly and focused manner."

Don Fites, CEO, Caterpillar, Inc.
1990 – 1999

"This was the late '80s. We'd experienced a decade without really any shareholder value being created . . . *survival* was a word we talked about around here.

"I think the DPI process was exactly the right approach to take because ours is a company where most of the people spend their lifetimes. We're very attached to the business and the equipment. We know the market and the customers. We know the business very well, and it's not a business that is easy to grasp. I mean, there aren't a whole lot of companies . . . there aren't really *any* companies in the world like Caterpillar. We don't have any models to follow. Forcing us to do that assessment process was exactly the right thing because only we, in the end, could have made that assessment, arrived at the conclusions, and took the path that we eventually did.

"I think the whole idea of someone from the outside telling people who have spent their whole lives in a company that something will or won't work is not really a good idea. They don't have the insight into what makes the company tick. The thing this process does very well, and I've seen it done over and over, is it forces you to come up with the good news and the bad news. And *you* find the answers to these issues yourselves.

"This is not a process for wimps. It is not a process where somebody is going to tell you how to save or maybe even improve your organization. But it is a process that if you go into it recognizing that you've got to change, that you've got to do better – if you want to maintain your leadership or *even survive* – this process, better than any I've seen, will get the job done.

"As far as the shareholders are concerned, the creation of shareholder value has been rather spectacular.

"I think it is one of the truly remarkable success stories of the 1990s. The track record is there in terms of financial results, market shares, percentage of sales . . . the whole nine yards."

Glen Barton, CEO, Caterpillar, Inc.
1999 to the Present

"We went through a number of consultants who worked with us. Among several others, we had the top strategy consultant at the time, Michael Porter, and Noel Tichy, who was a facilitator that had worked with General Electric on their break-out process . . . Rather than spending two or three years getting the background that a traditional strategy consultant like Porter might have wanted, we felt the DPI Process was a much more straightforward approach that we would be comfortable with and get faster results, which at the time was important.

"Some of these consulting projects never seem to end. They just keep rolling and rolling and getting bigger and bigger, and longer and longer, and more involved . . . In the last ten years we have used DPI's *Strategic Thinking Process* many times and when we undertake it we know there's an end. And when we get to that end, there are decisions we're going to make and directions we're going to take and move on from that.

"The Process drove us through considerations of what kind of company we wanted to be – product-driven, market-driven, or technology or manufacturing-driven. We finally arrived, through the process, at what we thought we were – and still are – a product-driven company.

"I think the reorganization is the most significant thing that has happened as a direct result of the DPI Process, and I think we had a total turnaround in our company in recent years as a result of it."

Which brings us to the most important concept in the *Strategic Thinking Process*, and the subject of the next chapter, the concept of Driving Force.

6

The Driving Force: The Engine of Competitive Supremacy

**"The Driving Force
is the DNA of strategy."**

To achieve competitive supremacy, a company needs to have a strategy that establishes a significant and sustainable point of differentiation – one that enables it to add *unique* value that competitors will have difficulty duplicating. Of course, most companies have a strategy of some sort. Yet few are able to create a clear definition of that single differentiating factor – if it has one – that has enabled it to be successful in the past. Still fewer have looked down the road to create a scenario – or strategy – that will enable them to do so in the environment it will face *in the future.*

We call that defining factor the Driving Force. It is the component of the business that is *unique to that company* and is the key determinant of the choices management makes with regard to future products, future customers, and future markets. Without an understanding of and agreement on that Driving Force, management will have a difficult time in creating a supremacy strategy for the future.

What Makes Your Strategy Tick?

The best way to determine if a CEO and the management team have a strategy is to observe them in meetings as they try to decide whether or not to pursue an opportunity. When we sat in on such meetings, what we observed was that management would put each opportunity through a hierarchy of different filters. The ultimate filter, however, was always whether there was a fit between the products, customers, and markets that the opportunity brought and *one* key component of the organization. If they found a fit there, they would feel comfortable with that opportunity, and would proceed with it. If they did not find a fit there, they would pass.

Different companies, however, looked for *different kinds* of fit. Some companies looked for a fit between similar products. Others were less concerned about the similarity of products than about a fit with the customer base. Still others were not interested in the similarity of products or of the customer base, but rather a fit with the technology involved, or a fit with its sales and marketing method, or its distribution system. Some quick examples.

What fit was Daimler looking for when it bought Chrysler? Obviously, the fit was one between similar products. Johnson & Johnson, on the other hand, looked for an entirely different kind of fit when it acquired Neutrogena creams from one company and the clinical laboratories of Kodak, each bringing dramatically different products. J&J was looking for a fit between the class of customers served – doctors, nurses, patients, and mothers – the heartbeat of J&J's strategy. 3M looked for still another fit when choosing opportunities. 3M did not care what the products were or who the customers were. What 3M did care about was whether there was a fit between the technology that the opportunity required and the technology – polymer chemistry – that lay at the root of 3M's strategy. If the technology fit, then 3M management felt comfortable in pursuing that opportunity.

Ten Strategic Areas

The next question that came to our minds was: "What are the areas of an organization that cause management to decide how to allocate resources or choose opportunities?" We discovered that each of the four hundred-plus companies we had worked with consisted of ten basic components.

- Every company offered a **product** or **service** for sale.

- Every company sold its product(s) or service(s) to a certain **class of customer** or **end user.**

- These customers or end users always resided in certain **categories of markets.**

- Every company employed **technology** in its product or service.

- Every company had a **production facility** located somewhere that had a certain amount of **capacity** or certain in-built **capabilities** in the making of a product or service.

- Every company used certain **sales** or **marketing methods** to acquire customers for its product or service.

- Every company employed certain **distribution methods** to get a product from its location to a customer's location.

- Every company made use of **natural resources** to one degree or another.

- Every company monitored its **size** and **growth** performance.

- Every company monitored its **return** or **profit** performance.

As a result of these observations, two key messages emerged. First, all ten areas exist in every company. Second, and more importantly, *one* of the ten areas tends to *dominate* the strategy of a company consistently over time. It is to favor or leverage this one area of the business time and again that determines how management allocates resources or chooses opportunities. In other words, one component of the business is the *engine* of the strategy – that company's so-called DNA, or Driving Force. This Driving Force determines the array of products, customers, industries, and geographic markets that management chooses to emphasize more and emphasize less.

Every Business Has 10 Components

... Which Determine Its Business Profile

... Because the Choices You Make About Products, Customers, And Markets Are Very *Different* For Each Driving Force

Strategic Profile

Driving Force: Supremacy's Propeller

In order to explain this concept more clearly, one needs to look at an organization as a *body in motion*. Every organization, on any given day, is an organism that has movement and momentum and is going forward in some direction. Our thesis is that one of the ten components of a company's operation is the strategic engine behind the decisions that management makes. Some typical examples follow.

Strategy Driven by Product

A company that is pursuing a *product*-driven strategy has deliberately decided to limit its strategy to a singular product and its derivatives. Therefore, all future products and the "current" product are linear, genetic extrapolations of the very first product that company ever made. In other words, the look, form, or function of the product stays constant over time. Examples of product-driven companies include Coca-Cola (soda), Boeing (airplanes), Michelin (tires), Harley-Davidson (motorcycles), and many of the automobile manufacturers (GM, Toyota, Volkswagen).

Strategy Driven by a User or Customer Class

A company that is driven by a *user* or *customer class* has deliberately decided to restrict its strategy to a describable and circumscribable class of end users or customers (people). These end users or customers are the only ones the company serves. The company then identifies a common need of the user or customer class and responds with a wide array of genetically unrelated products. Examples here include Johnson & Johnson (doctors, nurses, patients, and mothers), AARP (adults over 50), Playboy ("entertainment for men") and USAA (military officers).

Strategy Driven by Market Type or Category

A company that is driven by *market category* has deliberately decided to limit its strategy to a describable marketplace or market type. The company identifies a common need among buyers in that market and then responds with a wide variety of genetically unrelated products. Examples are American *Hospital* Supply (now Allegiance) and Disney's concept of "wholesome entertainment for the *family*."

Strategy Driven by Technology

A *technology*-driven company is rooted in some basic, hard technology, such as chemistry or physics, or some soft technology, such as know-how or expertise. The company then goes looking for applications for its technology or expertise. Once it finds an application, the company develops a product that is infused with its technology for that application, and offers the new product to all the customers in that market with a similar application. While growing that business, the company goes around looking for another application to repeat the same process. Examples of companies driven by technology are DuPont (chemistry), 3M (polymers), and Intel (microprocessor architecture).

Strategy Driven by Production Capability or Capacity

A company driven by production *capacity* is one which has a substantial investment in its production facility. The key phrase heard around the company is "keep it humming" – three shifts per day, seven days per week, 365 days per year. The strategy is to keep the production facility operating at a maximum level of capacity. Examples are steel companies, refineries, and pulp-and-paper companies.

A company driven by production *capability* has incorporated some distinctive capabilities into its production process that allow it to do things to its products that its competitors have difficulty duplicating. As a result, when the company goes looking for opportunities, it restricts its search to opportunities where these capabilities can be exploited. Specialty converters in a variety of industries are good examples.

Strategy Driven by Sales or Marketing Method

When a strategy is driven by a *sales* or *marketing method*, the company has a unique or distinctive method of selling to its customers. All the opportunities it pursues must utilize that selling method. Examples are companies that sell door-to-door (Avon, Mary Kay, and Amway), direct-response companies (Dell and K-tel), and catalog companies (L.L. Bean and Land's End). A recent addition is amazon.com, whose strategy is to use the Internet to sell a wide array of consumer products.

Strategy Driven by Distribution Method

A company driven by a *distribution method* has a unique or distinctive approach of moving tangible or intangible things from one place to another. All the opportunities such a company pursues must optimize that distribution method. Examples are Wal-Mart, FedEx, Home Depot, Staples, and Nextel.

Strategy Driven by Natural Resources

A company whose entire purpose is the pursuit and exploitation of oil, gas, ore, gold, timber, or other resources can be said to be pursuing a *natural resource*-driven strategy. Examples are Exxon, Shell, Newmont Gold, and Anglo-American Mining.

Strategy Driven by Size or Growth

A company driven by *size* or *growth* is usually a conglomerate of unrelated businesses. Its sole strategic interest is growth and size for their own sake.

Strategy Driven by Return or Profit

A company whose sole strategic focus is a minimum level of *return* or *profit* is also a conglomerate of unrelated businesses. The best example during the 1970s was ITT under Harold Geneen. His dictum of "an increase in quarterly earnings, every quarter, from every unit, regardless what" led ITT into 276 different businesses. These businesses were deliberately kept separate so that when any one unit missed its profit target for three consecutive quarters, it was gone in the fourth! Other examples are Tyco, AlliedSignal, and General Electric, where Jack Welch's dictum of an 18 percent ROA landed GE into everything from light bulbs to television networks to financial services to turbines and aircraft engines.

Key Strategic Questions

When we take a client through our *Strategic Thinking Process*, we have the CEO and the management team debate three key questions to enable them to identify the company's *current* and *future* Driving Force.

QUESTION 1: Which component of your business is currently *driving* your strategy and has made you look as you look today in terms of current products, customers, and markets?

If there are ten people in the room, how many answers do you think we get? Ten and sometimes more. The reason is simple. Each person has a different perception as to which component of the business is the Driving Force behind the company's strategy. These different interpretations lead to different visions of where the organization is headed. The difficulty, while this is going on, is that each member of the team makes decisions that pull the company left and right, so the company zigzags its way forward without establishing supremacy in any one sandbox. The inevitable result is that resources are wrongly employed.

The methodology we bring to bear at DPI encourages management to look back at the history of decisions they have made and, by doing so, recognize a pattern. Typically, most of their decisions were made to favor *one* component of the business. Thus, the management team recognizes the *current* Driving Force behind their *current* strategy.

QUESTION 2: Which component of the company *should* be the Driving Force behind the company's strategy in the *future*?

This question is more important, because it indicates that the company's future strategy should not be an extrapolation of the current strategy. Any strategy needs to accommodate the environment the company will encounter in the future, and that environment could be very different from the one encountered in the past. This question is the basis for envisioning "breakaway" strategies that explode the assumptions of the current sandbox to envision a new one that offers significantly greater opportunities to establish supremacy over competitors. Such a strategy enables the company to create, or reposition itself in, a future sandbox in a way that offers it more growth and profitability than that of competitors, and control of that sandbox.

QUESTION 3: What impact will this Driving Force have on the choices the company must make regarding future products, future customers, and future markets?

The Driving Force the company chooses as the engine of its strategy will determine the choices its management makes as to the products, customers, and markets that they *will* and *will not emphasize* in the future. These choices will shape the profile of the company, and maybe even the industry, over time. Each Driving Force will cause management to make very different choices that will make the company look very differently from the way it looks today. In other words, just as your personal DNA determines what you look like and why you look different from other people, the same is true for your corporate DNA. The component of the company you select as the DNA of its strategy will determine what that company will eventually look like and why it will look different from its competitors.

Fundamental Concept Of Competitive Supremacy

The concept of Driving Force, to us at DPI, is one that is *fundamental* for any successful CEO to understand. It is the recognition and understanding, by all members of the management team, of that *one* predominant component of the business – its Driving Force – that will allow the organization to formulate a strategy based on a *distinctive* and *sustainable advantage* that can give it supremacy over its competition. This enables the company to create new value from sources its competitors will have great difficulty duplicating.

Getting agreement on a single Driving Force is not an easy task. The following questions raised by CEOs and their management teams reveal the reasons why.

Does Your Strategy Suffer From The "Sybil Syndrome?"

"I can think of four or five strategic areas present in our business and they are of equal importance." In other words, there are *multiple* Driving Forces at work in the company. When we present the concept of Driving Force to CEOs for the first time, this is usually the first reaction that we get. We call it the "Sybil Syndrome." Do you remember the movie *Sybil*, about a woman with multiple personalities? Do you think that she had an easy time living with herself? Of course not! Every morning when she awoke, she did not know who she was. The same can be true of a company.

If multiple strategic areas are at the root of a company's strategy, and these strategies are regarded as equally important, the organization will develop multiple personalities and won't be able to tolerate itself. Even worse, it will have no basis for determining where to invest its resources to greatest advantage. The following strategy statement, from a real company, is a good example.

> "The Corporation strives to be a profitable and growing global manufacturer and marketer of value-added chemicals, an innovative supplier of niche life insurance and annuity products, and an increasingly significant force in the pharmaceutical industry."

The company? The Ethyl Corporation. When was the last time you saw this company mentioned as having supremacy in any of these sandboxes? In fact, the company performed so poorly and had such difficulty living with itself that it eventually divided into *four* separate public companies.

Does Your Strategy Suffer From Schizophrenia?

"If there cannot be multiple business areas driving our strategy, then I can identify two components in our company, equally important, that work in tandem." We call this the "schizophrenic strategy." One day you are in *this* mode, the next day you are in *that* mode. And the company zigzags its way forward, bouncing from one questionable opportunity to another. The problem with this kind of strategy is that resources are often dispersed or diluted and internal battles for them are waged on the basis of politics, not on a common understanding of the best opportunity to succeed over the long run.

Our contention is that, at any one moment in time, every organization has a *single* business component that is the Driving Force behind its strategy. Until members of the management team determine which component that is, they will have frequent disagreements over the allocation of resources and the choice of sound opportunities to pursue. Conversely, if management *is* in agreement on the Driving Force, decisions are made throughout the organization that focus resources on the best opportunities – and *not* on others.

Proof of this comes from the experiences of OM Group, a highly successful specialty chemical company that has used DPI's *Strategic Thinking Process* extensively. OM has honed a very sharp edge on the line of demarcation it uses to differentiate between opportunities. This is the direct result of its management's agreement on and adherence to a clearly defined Driving Force. Says CEO Jim Mooney:

"When our people develop products or look at markets, or identify acquisitions, they know what we're looking for. Now when they see an acquisition and they bring it to my attention they have already considered whether it fits in, whether it's metal-based specialty chemicals, whether it's something we can leverage with our production. We don't want to get into a me-too application. We look for new product potential, whether it offers new niches, whether it fortifies current weaknesses or builds on strengths."

This approach has translated into consistently exceptional performance. For proof, take a look at OMG's growth in sales and earnings – and at its stock's performance over the past eight years.

Is Profit Not The Single Purpose Of A Company?

It is a well-known fact that people must eat in order to survive. If they don't eat, they will die, guaranteed! But surely the purpose of life is not eating. Surely, there must be another purpose to life than eating, although people must eat every day.

The same line of thinking applies to a company. Most businesses have another purpose in life than producing a profit, although whatever that Driving Force is, every strategy must produce those results. If a company is not profitable, it will die, guaranteed! However, profit is the *result* of the strategy, not its *objective*. Profit tells you whether your strategy is working or not, but profit is not usually *the* strategy.

Isn't Any Strategy Subject To Darwinism?

Doesn't every strategy evolve over time? In other words, doesn't a company start with a certain Driving Force and evolve naturally to a second Driving Force and then eventually to a third, and so forth? Could you not start as product-driven, then go to technology, and then to customer class? Isn't there a natural evolution over time?

The answer, generally, is no. A good strategy stays in place and works for an organization over a long period of time. Take, for example, Mercedes's concept of the "best-engineered car." This strategy was first articulated in 1888 and, from then until today, that concept has produced a profit

every single year. The same is true of Wal-Mart, Johnson &
Johnson, Disney, and several others. In fact, we would pro-
pose that the opposite is also true. If you feel that your strategy
needs to change frequently, that is a clear signal you don't
have one!

Are There Any Legitimate Reasons For Changing The Driving Force?

There are three instances when you might want to shift the
strategy and direction of your organization by deliberately
changing the underlying Driving Force of your current strategy.

The first occurs when your current strategy runs out of
growth. Growth, like profit, is a "given" in business. Any
company must grow to perpetuate itself. Therefore, when
your strategy starts sputtering and runs out of growth, you
have a *legitimate* reason to sit down with your team and
debate whether the time has come to change the historical
Driving Force behind your current strategy.

Most PC makers who were pursuing undifferentiated, me-
too Product-driven strategies are currently facing that situation today. After a decade of continuous growth in demand,
the market has fallen off dramatically and PCs have become
increasingly commoditized. Bad news for me-too competitors
with little to differentiate their products or marketing. When
the market was growing rapidly there was plenty of business
for everyone. Now these me-too competitors are scrambling
for a solution to their dilemma. Most are opting for the obvious – consolidation or simply going under. Too late for many
of them.

The second situation arises when you look down the
horizon and see a death threat. In other words, there is
something at the root of the company's strategy that could
make the current Driving Force obsolete. This is another,
extremely *legitimate* reason for calling a meeting to explore
changing the strategy and direction of the company. Such
might be the case for a company like Johnson & Johnson.
If anyone – that is, anyone other than J&J – ever invented
a wellness pill, that would be the end of J&J's strategy of

satisfying the "health needs of doctors, nurses, patients, and mothers." Then you would see J&J looking for other customer groups to satisfy with radically different products than it produces today. J&J executives, on the other hand, have looked down that horizon and don't see obsolescence as a very high probability, so they will stay with their current Driving Force and strategy.

A third possibility, and the key premise of this book, is that you again look down that horizon and, instead of seeing a death threat, you are able to envision a new way of doing business that changes the game in the sandbox you foresee your company in. This may – but will not necessarily – require a change of Driving Force. A good example is LandAmerica, which is described in more detail in another chapter. LandAmerica was pursuing a Product-driven strategy – selling title insurance – a strategy that allowed them little differentiation or growth. Yet they envisioned the opportunity to change the game by placing themselves at the center of a variety of services related to real estate transactions – simplifying the process of real estate closings for realtors and attorneys. This required them to develop a new set of skills on top of their title insurance expertise and led them to change their Driving Force to being Market-driven, serving the "closing" needs of the real estate market. This change has enabled them to create a brand new sandbox, which, as their strategy is deployed, offers much broader opportunities to attain supremacy and generate superior returns.

Does Your Strategy Succumb To Seduction?

Alongside these legitimate reasons for changing the Driving Force and strategy of a company are factors that cause the strategy to change by *accident and not by design.* Management gets seduced by opportunities! An opportunity comes along and management, looking only at the numbers, concludes that it cannot afford not to be in that business. The company then pursues the opportunity because of the numbers, only to discover later that the opportunity has another Driving Force at its root. Before long, opportunity starts pulling the whole company off course. Has your company ever fallen prey to this kind of temptation?

When Is Seduction At Its Peak?

A company's management succumbs to seduction when its current strategy is so successful that it is generating more cash than the business needs. And the company starts accumulating excess cash.

Ford Motor Company is a good recent example. When Henry Ford first opened his plant in 1908, his strategy was clear: mass-produce a car that could be easily bought by the common man. At the time, this strategy was revolutionary, an unexpected supremacy strategy that changed the game. It was widely assumed, even by many of Ford's backers, that the rich were the best market for automobiles. After all, the rich had the money. The dozens of other new entrants into this incipient industry were all fighting over that turf. Yet Ford saw a future that no one else saw in which *everyone* would drive cars. Turns out he was right.

Of course, others eventually imitated Ford's strategy, yet for many decades, the company was one of the surest investments one could make. Ford followed a Product-driven strategy – making and selling cars and trucks – that it stuck to steadfastly through most of the twentieth century... until recently.

In January 2002, new CEO William Clay Ford, Jr., announced the closing of four plants, the discontinuation of four models, and the layoff of some 35,000 people. This occurred only after an extended period in which Ford's market share eroded and its stock price languished well below those of its key U.S. competitors.

What happened to sap Ford's dominance? In our view, they simply had fallen victim to seduction and gradually drifted from their Driving Force under CEO Jacques Nasser. Getting into businesses *apparently related* to cars, it acquired Hertz, Kwik-Fit (a chain of U.K. repair shops), and several others. The company, consciously or not, was drifting into a Market-Type or User-Class driven strategy, yet didn't make the kinds of changes in its management, structure, or expertise necessary to pursue such a strategy effectively. Ford didn't understand those businesses and neglected to nurture its strength – producing and selling cars and trucks. In his December 2001 presentation to analysts the incoming CEO said simply, "We strayed from what got us to the top of the mountain, and it cost us."

Whether the ancillary businesses were the direct cause of Ford's problems is debatable, but they were at best a distraction from its core business. As the *Wall Street Journal* reported at the time, CEO Ford said that, "Ultimately, the company's turnaround must be driven by developing cars and trucks people want to buy."

Strategy By Design, Not By Accident

The purpose of the *Strategic Thinking Process* is to help a company's CEO and management team make *conscious* decisions whose rationale and underlying logic are clearly understood. Understanding what the company does best – its *Driving Force* – and making it the engine of its strategy is the key skill of management. Once management agrees on the "engine," they are then able to formulate and deploy a distinctive strategy that can be leveraged to achieve supremacy over its competitors.

The concept of Driving Force is pivotal to the process and sets the stage for all future decisions.

Focus, Focus, Focus

The key to supremacy is simple: "Singularity of purpose, total dedication to it, and no deviation from it." This mantra demands that the strategy be kept strong and healthy, which, in turn, requires the nurturing of what we call "Areas of Excellence." The Driving Force chosen as the "strategic engine" will greatly alter the Areas of Excellence that a company must continually enhance if it wants to amplify the supremacy gap over its competitors. Understanding the relationship between the Driving Force and the corresponding Areas of Excellence allows management to deploy the company's energy and resources and enable it to *focus, focus, focus* and invest scarce resources where they will consistently drive that company toward its goal of competitive supremacy.

A good example of such a company is Southwest Airlines whose "mantra" is pure and simple:

"Thirty Years. One Mission. Low Fares."

That company has not deviated from that strategy since its origins in 1971 and has been building towards supremacy over its competitors ever since.

Another example is RasterGraphics, whose story is told in full in a later chapter of the book. Raster is a DPI client whose recognition of its Product Driving Force propelled it to the top of its market, eventually causing much larger competitors – Xerox and a division of Lockheed – to abandon the business. Said CEO Rak Kumar:

> "Our strategy was simple, yet it gave us enormous focus, and we never deviated from that. We defined our Driving Force as Product – wide format printers. Then we defined our Areas of Excellence as Product Development, and Sales and Service. That focus allowed us to introduce a series of new products at a pace that the others could not keep up with. It was that simple concept that set us on the path to supremacy in our sandbox."

Areas of Excellence? Those are the "boosters" that keep the Driving Force strong and healthy and widen the gap between the company and its competitors. We will explore the concept of Areas of Excellence in Chapter 7.

CEO Interview

Benjamin Salzmann
Chief Executive Officer
ACUITY

"We had a very strong debate over whether we should be Distribution-driven or Product-driven."

– Benjamin Salzmann

Two thousand one was a big year for ACUITY. It was the year they broke into the *A.M. Best 100 Largest Insurance Companies* list, and Ward named them one of the *50 Best Run Companies.* Other, perhaps even more significant, awards followed. All this in one of the most difficult insurance environments in recent memory. To understand why these honors are so remarkable, one only needs to look back a few years to when the company, then called Heritage, was one of the industry's most chaotic and inconsistent performers.

"In 1995," says CEO Ben Salzmann, "our combined ratio was 116, ten points higher than the industry."

The combined ratio is a key measure of an insurance company's profitability – percentage of premiums paid back in losses, plus agent commissions plus expenses. The break-even point before investment income is 100. The higher the number, the less profitable.

"Prior management grew the company over thirty years," Salzmann says. "I'll give them credit for that, but it happened in a very tumultuous way. It was always zig-zagging from profit to loss. There would be great growth with horrible losses, then a period of raising prices to get profitability back, but at the cost of huge chunks of market share. Market share dropped a full one-third in 1997. Think of the turmoil a company goes through when it loses a third of its sales. And we had become infamous with our agents for this pronounced inconsistent behavior. One effect was that we were severing relations with some of our best agents – our distribution channel. And to make matters worse, product development solely consisted of creating products suggested by a few agents, even if none of the other agents were interested in it or it wasn't profitable for the company."

Partly because of all this tumult, and partly because of work rules, morale at Heritage was at an all-time low. As Salzmann says, "If you told people you worked at Heritage, the reaction was always 'Why?' It was so bad, we even had bells that went off to tell you when you could take a break."

Clearly things had to change. And they did. When management transitioned in 1997, Ben Salzmann's charge was to create a focus on "profitable growth, where the word *profit* came through," as Salzmann puts it. This called for very fundamental changes in the way business was done – relationships with agents, product offerings – the very culture of the company. To help develop a clear direction among the management team, they decided to bring in an outside firm to help them create a new strategy.

"We brought in about a half dozen planning companies at least twice on site. We did reference checks. We went through their methodologies. If they wrote books we bought the books, read them, critiqued them. We created, I would say, a five hundred-page three-ring binder comparing content planning versus process and then critiquing the various consultants. What we liked about DPI was that while they had an academically justifiable process, they didn't get lost in academia. In all their books and materials, they immediately took the theory and made it very pragmatic, constantly tying their methodology into case studies with real results. We had the full professors with Ph.D.s from the various big business schools in here talking about content planning, with their incredible rhetoric. But we kept saying, 'Show us your clients and what you actually did for them. And show us how it made a difference within their industries.' Whereas every piece of material from DPI said, '*This* is our client in *this* industry. This is how our process helped them find another way to conduct their business. And this is how it benefited them.' DPI kept tying the theory and processes back into real cases of clients in the practical business environment and the end results they achieved.

"We also learned the difference between content and process strategy consultants. With DPI *we* do the thinking using their process. *Content* planners arrive with the most recent Spring graduates and one semi-seasoned planner who's billed out at a horrific rate. They come in and do 'meatball surgery.' They leave you to figure out what to do next. With DPI *we* create the strategy and there's a clear timetable and responsibilities for implementation. It just made more sense to us. With DPI we also knew we would be working with an experienced veteran, Mark Thompson. He commands your attention and our officers respected him. A lot of strategic planners don't get that kind of respect because their methodologies don't work and their strategies never get implemented."

ACUITY's management assembled a team from across the company to go through the process.

"Mark told us we needed to have representation from throughout the company to get the maximum buy-in. We had been building a culture that involves people in decision making so that immediately dovetailed with who we are. He also said, 'Look for rising stars, such as an underwriter who you see growing with the company. They bring frontline exposure. Take advantage of that.' Those things matched our culture. It was a natural fit."

As the process progressed in the first three-day session, a

major revelation emerged that would lead to significant shifts in how the company did business. After extensive debate over the company's Driving Force, the team realized that they had been Distribution-driven *by default.* In other words, the distribution system – its agents, and actually only a portion of them – were dictating everything from product development to commission structure to geographic reach.

As Salzmann recalls, "We had a very strong debate over whether we should be Distribution-driven – where it is the agent that drives us – or whether we should be Product/Service-driven. We were defaulting under previous management to giving away the selection of future products and marketing and sales to our *agents.* That doesn't mean we don't value our agents – we do. They are our lifeblood, a vital link to our customers. We listen to them very carefully. But *we* should be developing the products because that's our expertise, *and* we underwrite the risk.

"The agent's job is to bring us together with potential insureds. But we had been listening to anecdotal evidence from individual agents and developing products that the majority of agents didn't want. An agent might also say, 'I'm on the border of this particular state and I want to write business there,' and we'd go into a new state without ever looking to see if that would be profitable for us. We should have been doing the research across many agents, and across the marketplace to develop products that meet the needs of the majority of agents – and *us.* In the end, as a result of recognizing our Product/Service Driving Force, we decided to completely reorient the organization, taking back ownership of marketing, sales, product development, communications."

Out of the process came a list of eight Critical Issues that would begin to make this major change in their business. Issues such as increasing the pace of e-commerce, taking ownership of marketing and sales, customer-direct service, data utilization – even a communications program that involved changing the company name to signify the depth of changes taking place – were created and assigned to individuals to manage to completion.

One of the Critical Issues involved moving the responsibility for service from the agents back to ACUITY. This has accomplished two ends. It relieves agents of a complex task for which they are not compensated, and also provides a means for ACUITY to create direct links to its customers, thereby strengthening those relationships, and developing brand loyalty. Most of all, it enables ACUITY to leverage an Area of Excellence it now nurtures to support its Driving Force.

"Superior service in insurance isn't just getting the customer something faster," Salzmann explains. "Superior service means things like helping your customer with loss control. You could save 8 percent this year by going with Acme, and have more losses and wind up paying 30 percent more in premiums the following year. We now help commercial customers to *reduce* losses, which lowers their premiums. That's just one of the ways we can provide value-added service and really please the customer."

One of the most important Critical Issues was the creation of *new* products and services. These could range from new types of insurance to new services to the customer.

To catalyze this effort they decided to use DPI's *Strategic Product Innovation Process* (SPI). This process applies a systematic approach to flushing out new ideas, and then allows participants to filter them against a matrix of strategic fit, ease of implementation, risk/reward, and various other measures. The result is a short list of concepts that further the strategic goals outlined in the *Strategic Thinking Process.* Additionally, an integral output is a practical implementation plan with timelines to assure crisp development and rollout.

"The whole idea of using this process was to get fresh, new ideas from across the whole company," says Laura Conklin, ACUITY's Vice President of Business Consulting, who has headed up the product development effort. "We brought in a group of people from all levels and parts of the company, people who we identified as having a lot of drive and openness, to bring out ideas that might have been stifled in the past."

Out of the SPI sessions came a series of innovative services and products. Some are as simple as online availability of Certificates of Insurance for contractors. This helps the contractor to get the certificate quickly, relieves the agent of having to drop everything to deliver it, provides a link to the end customer that helps strengthen the relationship, and streamlines the process of being a customer.

Other products are actual insurance products, one of which is a major innovation designed for the next time a "soft market" occurs.

Understandably reluctant to provide details, Salzmann explains, "We came up with an outstanding new product. We're timing its release for the next period when commercial rates start to fall again – a soft market. This product will be tremendous in counterbalancing the commercial insurance market when we go from the present hard market, where rates are at a premium, to a soft market where we can't get enough for the risks we're assuming. That's the most important time to have a strategy and the DPI processes have helped us to get to products like this that are crucial to our 'profitable growth' objective."

The development of such profit-making products and services has become part of ACUITY's modus operandi. Says Conklin, "The DPI process has got us thinking this way all the time now. We don't even think of new product development as a Critical Issue anymore. It's become part of our culture. It's how we work."

The results of the new strategy have been steady and impressive. "Remember," says Salzmann, "the challenge was to grow premiums and remain profitable, and to have our agents respect us again, to be able to say to them, 'We will be profitable and grow and not disappear on you.' Now, at the end of 2001 we were wonderfully profitable. Here's an example. The whole industry's combined ratios (remember, lower is better) have risen from 105.6 in 1998 to 117 in 2001; ours have gone from 99.9 to 101.8 in the same period – 15.2 points more profitable than the industry. Add in our investment income and we made $7 million. That's really incredible. And what about premiums! In 1997 it was $225 million. At the end of 2001 it was $425 million, so we grew by $200 million. Our anticipated premium at the end of 2002 is $500 million. We've cleaned up the way the company was doing business, become consistently profitable, and stopped the zig-zagging."

As to the awards ACUITY has received, Salzmann is justifiably pleased. "The one I'm most proud of is making the *Fortune 100 Best Places To Work,* considering what our reputation was just four years ago," he says.

"Second, remember I said that we were formerly running as a Distribution-driven organization, where Distribution means our agents, and then changed to Product/Service-driven. Ironically, since we've made that change to Product-driven, we're doing a better job for our agents. The National Professional Independent Agents voted ACUITY the *Best Insurance Company* in the nation – the singular best. That means we're rated above all the big-name insurance companies whose names you know! I think that's just amazing. Because we recognized our true Driving Force and did it better, our distribution channel named us *the* top insurance company in the nation.

"On top of that, Ward, which rates all three thousand insurance companies doing business in the United States, named us to the *50 Best Run Companies* in 2001 and 2002. And as if all that's not enough, ACORD, which rates technology use, named us *Technology Champion.*

"But the real rewards come from customers. The numbers speak for themselves."

CEO Interview

Peter Samoff
President & Chief Operating Officer
T. D. Williamson, Inc.

> **"We *knew* we were Technology-driven . . .
> and we had probably become, over many, many
> years, more of a *Product*-driven company . . .
> We *decided* to shift our Driving Force
> to Customer Class."**
>
> *– Peter Samoff*

For several decades, T.D. Williamson, Inc., has been the worldwide leader in pigs. No, not that kind of pig. These are specialized pigs, equipment that cleans and measures the geometry of a pipeline. Beginning with pigs, this eighty-year-old privately-held company has developed equipment to perform maintenance, without shutdown, on under-pressure piping systems. The company is the recognized leader in hot tapping and plugging products and services worldwide. Business had been good; the company was stable. But management realized that significantly greater growth was essential if they wanted to remain so. Yet efforts to charge up the engine had fallen short of where they wanted to be.

"We had few competitors and we certainly had the lion's share of the business that we were in," says Pete Samoff, President and COO of the privately-held Tulsa, Oklahoma company. TDW currently has about seven hundred employees living in twenty different countries. "We're the company that developed the technologies and marketed them, bringing something to the pipeline marketplace that's truly needed, and we're highly respected for the quality of our work. But the market for those products was getting mature. The company could only grow at the rate of the market segment. We had done all the right things to find new growth – searching out new markets, pushing the organization for growth. We ran harder, invested capital, developed new markets. We did all those things but really couldn't outpace the market itself. We just weren't getting the *level* of growth that we felt we needed as a company.

"We also wanted to see a company that would look more for opportunities, a company that would be more aggressive, that would assume a little more risk in the way we approach things. Not risk in the marketplace, not risk in what we do as a company, because you can't have risk when you're working on live gas pipelines. I'm talking about that risk that would enable people to say, 'Okay, I think this is a good idea and we should pursue it and I'm willing to go forward with it.' And that just wasn't something that we had."

Samoff and his top managers had tried to tackle the issue of growth, or lack of it, in their annual strategic planning meetings, but they didn't seem to be able to break out of their current business's confines.

Says Samoff, "I had been President for three years, and when I looked at what we'd accomplished in these planning meetings over that time frame, I realized we'd gone over the same issues every year, and they were much more operational than strategic in nature. We really needed to get beyond that. That's when we set out to find somebody who could bring some discipline to the process, to get us on the strategic side of things and off the operational issues."

After a thorough search of strategy consulting options, the DPI *Strategic Thinking Process* rose to the top, as it represented a means to mine the knowledge and experience of TDW's own managers, collectively amounting to hundreds of man-years. The process, which systematically extracts a complete picture of the company, its products, markets, and view of the future business arena, would allow them, they felt, to draw on their deep understanding, to envision a new future for T.D. Williamson, Inc.

"The fact that the DPI process uses *our* people to develop *our* strategy, that it's not people coming in and doing it *for* us made a whole lot of difference," Samoff states. In assembling the group that would go through the process, Samoff and his senior managers were interested in extracting the best thinking of a diverse cross-section of the company. "We brought in thirty-five people from ten different countries, people with different backgrounds, and different markets – some from developing markets and others from markets that were very mature."

DPI Partner George Spiva facilitated the process, keeping the discussion on track and assuring that all points of view would be heard. Says Samoff, "I think having a facilitator like George Spiva, who's experienced at this process, was important. An outside facilitator makes sure that you stick to the program and that the most vocal or most senior people don't take over the discussion."

As they went through the sequence of the process, they quickly found that this crossbreeding of ideas led to lively debate, with new perspectives emerging. "It was interesting to see how, in fact, we didn't always agree on everything, but in the end we came out with thirty-five people who were on board as to where we're heading."

The turning point came, as it often does, during the debate over their Driving Force, which, in the parlance of the DPI process, is the specific set of skills and capabilities at the core of the company that propels it toward a given set of products, customers, and markets.

The discussion at T.D. Williamson, Inc., brought about a surprising conclusion. Most of the team *thought* they were Technology or Know-How-driven – pipeline maintenance technology – but soon realized they had gradually *become* Product-driven – niche suppliers of equipment and services – and determined they *should* be Customer Class-driven – offering solutions for the maintenance needs of owners/operators of pressurized piping systems.

Samoff describes the discussion this way, "When we got into the Driving Force we all *knew* we were a Technology/Know-How-driven company – the Know-How being the specialized ability to service pressurized pipes. We'd been doing it for eighty years. But when we got into talking about it – and we did have some heated discussions – all of a sudden we began to question if that's who we truly were. It was interesting to watch the discussion evolve as we realized that we had probably become, over many, many years, more of a *Product*-driven company and not what we *thought* we were. We were the market leader in hot tapping and plugging equipment for a long time, but after a time the equipment was in broad use. And we came to the conclusion that our customers weren't really looking for us to be just an equipment supplier any longer.

"So we found that who we thought we were, we really weren't, and realized our customers were looking for us to be more. So we decided to shift our Driving Force to Customer Class and expand the services we offer to our customer base. We already had most of the capabilities we needed to do that. But what we would really need to do to make this change was to develop a new Area of Excellence, and spend a lot of time with our customers to find out more about what they're doing and what else we can do to help them in their businesses."

As a result, the group hammered out a concise new Business Concept that would reshape the company and provide a blueprint for the future:

"We will anticipate and respond to the maintenance needs of owners and operators of pressurized piping systems with innovative solutions that leverage our unique operating and technical capabilities that have application in all of our geographic markets. By partnering with our customers we will enable them to minimize their risk and maximize utilization of their assets."

As Samoff explains, "There are about a half-dozen key words in there and our managers understand it. We use it as a filter for what we *will* and will *not* do."

To illustrate the difference between the new concept and old, Samoff recalls an incident that occurred a few years ago. "I was listening to one of our guys telling a customer how to go about doing a particular type of job. He was telling this engineer exactly what he needed to do to clean his pipeline, and how he needed to do it. That's just how we supported our customers who'd bought pigs. I think that pig sale was three or four thousand dollars. Today, we're doing the *whole* cleaning job, which could be $300,000, and the pig sale's still three thousand. So we really do it from beginning to end now, rather than just selling the products."

This has grown the field of opportunity dramatically, enabling T. D. Williamson, Inc., to drastically alter their view of the future possibilities.

"We've got a much larger sandbox, a much larger opportunity. Now we're in the process of learning more and more about our customers. We need to understand them well enough, so that when they're out there trying to decide what to do next and they get to a decision about where *they* want to be, we're already standing there ready to serve. That's where *we* want to be."

Critical Issues: A Pipeline To Implementation

As any CEO knows, creating a strategy is only the first step. A crucial step, but only the beginning. Making sure it happens requires a disciplined approach, the backbone of which is a list of Critical Issues – an essential output of DPI's *Strategic Thinking Process.*

"The greatest thing about it for me," Samoff says, "was that we came out of the DPI process with a clear list of Critical Issues. Issues like customer research, maintaining our brand equity, breaking new markets. We had the people who took part in the strategy sessions design and pursue these. We have a lot of ownership in the process because a lot of people have been involved."

Samoff believes this *involvement* in these issues has been essential to getting commitment to the strategy and effective implementation.

"We selected the Critical Issue teams very carefully, and as time went on brought in more and more people. By the time we'd been through the first meeting or two, we had somewhere between eighty and a hundred people directly involved. That led to a lot of buy-in throughout the company around the *world* – and a focus on getting it done."

One of the most pressing Critical Issues was to prepare TDW's seven hundred people for the changes that would be taking place. After all, these highly skilled workers had been doing the same types of things for many years and the company seemed to be doing well, enjoying a sterling reputation in its field. Why change? Why now? How?

"One of the things we had to do was to change the culture in a company that really resisted change," Samoff explains. "Any kind of change caused a great deal of anxiety. In addition to directly involving people in the changes, one of the tools we used is a set of videos to explain change. In the first one, we used the lemonade stand to try to put the new strategy in terms everybody would understand. It was about a lemonade stand that only sold lemons and water and sugar, and you made your own lemonade, versus one that made the lemonade (complete solutions). Another video was about the Critical Issues, and another on progress and successes.

"Our personnel were told that there would be organizational changes and there were. We told people we were going to change who our customers were, that we were going to change how we do business, bring in new skills. And we did all those things. People are beginning to recognize that change is here, that it's going to happen, and they can see the positive results.

"Now when we're talking about making a change or coming up with a new breakthrough capability, people want to be a part of those teams, teams like the lean manufacturing team. They see that this new strategy is really what's *driving* where we're headed and they want to be a part of it. They now understand that change isn't necessarily bad, that change can make things better. This could never have happened two or three years ago. The process would have just faded away. Now when I walk through the shop and offices around the world, people all want to talk about the strategy and how we're doing, not just where the next order's coming from."

Another Critical Issue team's charge was user research – learning everything it could about relevant customer needs to flesh out future products and services. Another was assigned to researching and creating a plan to handle a burgeoning customer need, called pipeline integrity. "It's a new market that's emerged in the United States and we're there already. Ready to support our customers," Samoff says.

As these and other Critical Issues have progressed, the much needed growth has followed along exceptionally well.

"One of the things we said was that we wanted to *double* the size and value of the company in five years. That would have been a big stretch for our company historically," Samoff states.

"Right now, in the first full year of our new strategy, we're *way* ahead of where we thought we'd be. We've had a very good year – the best in our history. Our sales volume increased by 20 percent versus the typical 6 percent over the past several years. This put us ahead of our five-year target and expected revenue growth, and total company value is continuing to exceed our projections.

"We can actually measure and see how much of that growth has come from the new strategy and how much from our traditional market niche. So being able to pass that along to all of our people has been a real shot in the arm for everybody."

7

Areas of Excellence: Amplifying the Supremacy Gap

"Supremacy is not a dirty word."

Jeff Bezos, the CEO of amazon.com, eloquently articulated our concept of competitive supremacy with this statement:

> "Barnes & Noble and Borders are having trouble because it is hard to pursue me-too strategies online. In book retailing, amazon.com still does the best job, and not by a little. The gap between us and our competitors is significant and grows every quarter."

There are two interesting parts to this statement. First, the recognition that me-too strategies are not worth the paper they are written on and that only a strategy that is distinctive and sets you apart from your competitors will enable you to attain supremacy over them. The second interesting part of this statement is the notion that the "gap" between a company and its competitors can amplify over time. This "supremacy gap" is created and can amplify over time by the cultivation of what we call "Areas of Excellence."

An Area of Excellence is a specific *skill or capability* that a company *deliberately* nurtures to a higher level of proficiency than any other competitor because it is their superiority in these two or three capabilities that keeps their strategy strong and healthy and widens the supremacy gap over their competitors.

Some CEOs understand this concept and know exactly what the Areas of Excellence are that give the company its strategic advantage over its competitors.

David Glass, the recently retired CEO of Wal-Mart, said:

> "Our distribution facilities are the key to our success. If we do anything better than other folks, that's it."

Knowing that, Glass invested over a billion dollars during his reign on sophisticated computer systems to maintain and increase that supremacy gap.

Fred Smith, CEO of FedEx, also knows what contributes to its supremacy over its competitors:

> "The main difference between us and our competitors is that we have more capacity to track, trace, and control items in the system."

Determining The Strategic Capabilities That Amplify Supremacy

Product-Driven Strategy

A Product/Service-driven company survives on the quality of its product or service. Witness the automobile wars. Who's winning? The Japanese. Why have Americans been buying Japanese cars and even been willing to pay premium prices for the last forty years? The answer is simple: The Japanese make better cars. The bottom line for a Product-driven strategy is: best product wins! Raster Graphics achieved their stunning victory over two much larger competitors by pursuing this principle with an unwavering commitment.

One Area of Excellence, therefore, is *product development.* Compared to U.S. cars, Japanese cars of the late 1950s (when cars from Japan came onto the market) were far inferior. But Japanese car manufacturers understood well that "best car wins" and they strove to improve the product – to make it better and better – to the extent that Japanese cars eventually surpassed the quality of U.S. cars. Ford, traditionally Product-driven, is learning this lesson the hard way. Wandering into ancillary businesses diverted resources – and the company's attention – away from the constant drive to develop new and better cars. It has cost them their supremacy.

A second Area of Excellence is *service.* IBM, which also pursues a Product-driven strategy, is well aware of this requirement. Ask IBM clients what they admire most about IBM, and ninety-nine out of a hundred will say they admire its service capability. IBM deliberately invests more resources in its service function than any of its competitors, and thus has a considerable edge in response time and infrequency of product failures.

In a Product-driven mode, you amplify your supremacy by cultivating excellence in *product development* and *product service.*

Market Category/User Class-Driven Strategy

An organization that is Market Category or User Class-driven must also cultivate excellence to optimize its strategic supremacy, but in dramatically different areas.

A Market/User Class-driven company has placed its destiny in the hands of a *market category* or a *class of users.* Therefore, to survive and prosper, it must know its user class or market category better than any competitor. *Market* or *user research,* then, is one Area of Excellence. The company must know everything there is to know about its market or user in order to quickly detect any changes in habits, demographics, likes, and dislikes. Procter & Gamble interviews consumers (particularly homemakers) over two million times a year in an attempt to anticipate trends that can be converted into product opportunities.

A second Area of Excellence for a Market/User Class-driven company is *user loyalty.* Through a variety of means, these companies, over time, build customer loyalty to the company's products or brands. Then they trade on this loyalty. Over time, Johnson & Johnson has convinced its customers that its products are "safe." And it will not let anything infringe on the loyalty it has developed because of this guarantee. Whenever a Johnson & Johnson product might prove to be a hazard to health, it is immediately removed from the market.

Production Capacity/Capability-Driven Strategy

When there is a glut of paper on the market, the first thing a paper company does is lower the price. Therefore, to survive during the period of low prices, one has to have the lowest costs of any competitor. To achieve this, *manufacturing or plant efficiency* is a required Area of Excellence. This is why paper companies are forever investing their profits in their mills – to make them more and more efficient. An industry that has lost sight of this notion is the U.S. steel industry. By not improving their plants, they have lost business to the Italians and Japanese, who have done so. One notable exception in the United States is Nucor, which has done very well because it has the lowest costs of any steel mill, including the Japanese and Italian mills. As a result, Nucor's revenues and profits have consistently improved.

DPI client, Teckwah, a Singapore-based commercial printer, had traditionally been Production Capacity-driven. The company had done all it could to optimize its printing operations, yet realized that a saturated market allowed little growth. As Managing Director Thomas Chua said:

> "There's no point to trying to keep up the capacity if you don't have the business."

In going through the *Strategic Thinking Process,* the company decided to focus on a couple of industries and expand its range of services beyond printing. It, therefore, changed its Driving Force to being Market-driven and changed its Areas of Excellence to the ones described in the previous section.

A second Area of Excellence for the Production Capacity-driven strategy is *substitute marketing.* Capacity-driven companies excel at substituting what comes off their machines for other things. The paper people are trying to substitute paper for plastic; the plastic people are trying to substitute plastic for aluminum; concrete for steel. The same is true in the transportation industry where bus companies are trying to replace trains, and trains replace the airlines, and so forth.

A Production Capability-driven company is one that has built special capabilities into its production process that allow it to make products with features that are difficult for its competitors to duplicate. It then looks for opportunities where these capabilities can be exploited.

Job shops and specialty printers are examples. As a result, these companies are always looking to add to or enhance these distinctive production capabilities, because herein resides their competitive advantage.

Technology/Know-How-Driven Strategy

A company that is Technology-driven uses technology as its edge. Thus, an Area of Excellence required to win under this strategy is *research*, either basic or applied. Sony, for example, spends 10 percent of its sales on research, which is 2 or 3 percent more than any competitor. Its motto, "research is the difference," is proof that the company's management recognizes the need to excel in this area.

By pushing the technology further than any competitor, new products and new markets will emerge. Technology-driven companies usually *create* markets rather than respond to needs, and they usually follow their technology wherever it leads them.

A second Area of Excellence for Technology-driven companies is *applications marketing.* Technology-driven companies seem to have a knack for finding applications for their technology that call for highly differentiated products. For example, 3M has used its coating technology to develop Post-it® note pads and some sixty thousand other products.

Sales/Marketing Method-Driven Strategy

The prosperity of a Sales Method-driven company depends on the reach and effectiveness of its selling method. Dell, whose Driving Force is its direct response selling method, has the best website of all companies that use the Internet as their selling method.

The second Area of Excellence needed to succeed with this strategy is improving the *effectiveness* of the selling method. Dot-coms, such as Amazon and Priceline, are constantly improving their unique selling method – their websites. Door-to-door companies are constantly training their salespeople in product knowledge, product demonstration, and selling skills. Growth and profits come from improving volume through the diversity and effectiveness of its sales method.

Distribution Method-Driven Strategy

To win the war while pursuing a Distribution Method-driven strategy, you must first have the *most effective* distribution method. As a result, you offer only products and services that use or enhance your distribution system. Second, you must always look for ways to optimize the *effectiveness*, either in cost or value, of that system. That is your edge. You should also be on the lookout for any form of distribution that could bypass or make your distribution method obsolete.

Both FedEx and Wal-Mart are good examples of Distribution Method-driven companies. They are constantly striving to improve the efficiency of their respective distribution systems.

Natural Resource-Driven Strategy

Successful Resource-driven companies excel at doing just that – *exploring* and finding the type of resources they are engaged in.

John Bookout, ex-CEO of Shell USA, is a good example of a strategist who understood his company's Areas of Excellence. Shell's particular expertise is "enhanced oil recovery in offshore waters deeper than six hundred feet." In this area, Shell has few rivals, as Bookout explained. In the 1980s, Shell drilled a project called Bullwinkle in the Gulf of Mexico at a depth of 1350 feet. Outsiders thought the project was too risky, particularly since Shell did not spread the risk by taking other partners in on the deal. "You can't believe how easy that decision was," he said. "It took us thirty minutes in the boardroom." The reason? Bookout was banking on Shell's Area of Excellence in deep water recovery.

This Area of Excellence has enabled Shell to paralyze its competitors. Shell eventually announced major discoveries in the Gulf of Mexico that contain record quantities of oil. Even its competitors recognized this superiority. As Amoco

Areas Of Excellence
(Strategic Skill)

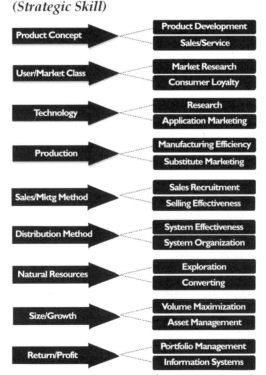

ex-CEO, Laurance Fuller, admitted then: "When it comes to deep water drilling, Shell is out in front of the industry."

Size/Growth Or Return/Profit-Driven Strategy

Companies that choose either a Size/Growth-driven or a Return/Profit-driven strategy require excellence in financial management. One such area is *portfolio management.* This means proficiency at moving assets around in order to maximize the size/growth or return/profit of the entire organization.

A second Area of Excellence is *information systems.* These companies usually have a corporate "Big Brother" group that constantly monitors the performance of its various divisions and as soon as a problem is detected, an attempt is made to quickly correct or expunge it so that the financial damage can be kept to a minimum.

The Concept Of Strategic Leverage

"Corporations don't compete, business units do." So says Michael Porter of the Harvard Business School in his book, *Competitive Advantage.* This conclusion is based on the notion that as a company grows into an array of multiple products and customer groups, it ends up in a variety of different markets, each with a different group of competitors. Thus the need, and the Porter rationale, to separate the corporation into business units based on a product/customer matrix that places each unit "closer to the market" and increases its ability to compete successfully.

In our view, nothing could be further from the truth. Our own experience with all four hundred of our clients clearly indicates the opposite phenomenon. It is *companies* that compete and *not* business units! In fact, what will determine a business unit's ability to compete (or not compete) is determined even before that business unit is formed.

Successful companies, in our view, are those that can leverage their unique set of capabilities – Driving Force and Areas of Excellence – across the largest number of products and markets. Companies that can spread the heartbeat of the business and their accompanying strategic capabilities across as many business units as possible are those that will assist that business unit in surviving and prospering. The opposite is also true. Business units that cannot use key corporate capabilities are often "orphaned" from the thrust of the corporation and will have difficulty making it on their own.

The Link Between Business Unit Success
And Corporate Competitiveness

Sharp, of Japan, is an excellent example of a company that has leveraged its unique capabilities. Sharp manufactures LCDs for laptop computers as well as a large number of other consumer electronic devices, ranging from cordless phones, projection televisions, and fax machines to electronic diaries and calculators. It has recently introduced laser diodes for use in computers, laser printers, CD players, and videodisc players. It is working on photosensitive films that will someday function as a self-contained image-processing computer and eliminate the need for memory chips and microprocessors.

Why is Sharp engaged in all these diverse product, customer, and market areas? They all draw on Sharp's knowledge of optoelectronic technology. "We've been accumulating optoelectronics know-how for thirty years," said President Haruo Tsuji, which accounts for Sharp's success as the world's largest supplier of optoelectronic devices with sales of over $100 billion annually. Sharp, in our opinion, has mastered this concept of capability leverage to the *nth* degree.

Canon is another example of a company that has mastered the concept of strategic leverage. Canon's wide range of products – copiers, cameras, and fax machines – all draw on that company's optics technology. Canon is also a good example of what happens when a company tries to innovate outside its strategic capabilities. In the mid-1980s, Canon made an enormous investment in the fast-growing and seductive PC market by introducing a PC of its own. Massive investment, massive failure. Why? Have you ever seen a PC with a lens? No lens, no probability of success. However, if Canon could figure out how to design a PC with a lens that makes it do things other PCs can't, like scanning, then it would probably have a winner.

Yet another Japanese company that clearly understands its heartbeat, or Driving Force, is Honda. Although its most visible products are its cars, Honda also makes lawn mowers, motorcycles, and generators. All these products revolve around Honda's key expertise – engines – and the company is religiously following Honda's business concept of "engines for the world." When Honda entered Formula 1 racing, it went in with its *engines*. The car bodies were by McLaren, Lotus, and others.

3M is probably the best example of a U.S. company that has built an array of more then sixty thousand products based on its knowledge of polymer chemistry as applied to coatings and adhesives. This strategic capability has led 3M into some fifty business arenas, such as film, floppy disks, videocassettes, audiotape, sandpaper, adhesive tape, electrical tape, and computer wires to Post-it® notes.

What has this leveraging led to for each of these companies? Supremacy in their respective sandboxes. Each has nurtured a specific set of capabilities to a degree far beyond its competitors and then spread those capabilities to each business unit. The result – a continuous stream of new-to-the-market products leading to competitive supremacy.

Leveraging Your Product Innovation Investment

As we worked with more and more companies over the years, we noticed that some got much more "bang for the buck" from their strategy efforts than others. For example, why is it that Merck can develop twelve new blockbuster prescription drugs in a ten-year period when the industry average is one every fifteen years?

The answer is simple. Those that have achieved supremacy over their competitors had clearly identified the Driving Force at the root of their strategy. They had also clearly identified the corresponding *strategic capabilities* that the company must excel at to allow their strategies to dominate those of their competitors.

The reason for Merck's success stems from ex-CEO Ray Vagelos's deliberate investment in four areas of medical science – biochemistry, neurology, immunology and molecular biology. All twelve of the blockbuster drugs were derived from these four strategic capabilities deliberately cultivated by Vagelos to a higher level of proficiency than any of its competitors.

Thus, our advice to our clients is that the best product innovation process is one that *leverages the company's strategic capabilities* and "fits" the strategy of the business.

We have also discovered that a company that attempts to innovate outside its strategic parameters – its Driving Force and accompanying Areas of Excellence – usually fails. And there is yet another good reason for that to occur: *Most innovations stem from existing knowledge that has yet to be commercially exploited.*

For example, it is not a coincidence that Edison and Siemens invented the light bulb, in different parts of the world, within hours of each other. Neither man would have done this if electric generation and the conduction of electricity through wire had not been invented first. Mr. Daimler and Mr. Benz would not have developed the automobile if the combustion engine had not been discovered first. Steve Jobs and Steve Wozniak would not have developed the personal computer if someone else had not discovered the microprocessor first. And the list goes on.

Leonardo da Vinci's prolific ideas are further proof of this notion. As brilliant a new product innovator as he was – he conceived the bicycle, the helicopter, and the submarine over four hundred years ago – the fact remains that most of his ingenious inventions never saw the light of day. One cannot build a helicopter without the prior knowledge of shaping flat metal. One cannot build a submarine without the prior knowledge of a means of providing oxygen to a vehicle submerged underwater.

The same is true of innovation within a company. Every company develops areas of knowledge and expertise that it adds to over time. Any new product innovation that draws on that knowledge has a high probability of success, whereas any that does not has a high probability of failure.

Thus, a company can leverage its new product innovation investment by favoring innovations that draw on the strategic heartbeat (Driving Force) and the accompanying strategic capabilities (Areas of Excellence) of the enterprise. In fact, *leveraging these across the broadest array of products and markets* is the key to a product innovation program that will outpace the competition and, thus, lead to competitive supremacy. Successful new product creation works like a telescope. It produces the best results when it derives from an extension of the company's Driving Force and Areas of Excellence to create new products for new markets.

Strategic Leverage

Understanding which component of the business is your strategic heartbeat and the corresponding strategic capabilities will greatly enhance your ability to succeed in your current markets. It will also open up other opportunities – in possibly unrelated product/market areas – that are strategically sound because they draw on the firm's Driving Force and Areas of Excellence.

Honda recently announced the development of a new car engine that meets the California emissions standards today – without the need to change anything about the gasoline or even having a catalytic converter. How long do you think it will be before Honda introduces this technology into its lawn mowers, chain saws, and tractors? Right! Twelve and a half seconds! Why? Simply because the competitive position of each of these business units will be enhanced by drawing on this corporate capability.

Strategic leverage means changing the equation that says $1 + 1 = 2$ into one that says $1 + 1 = 3$, sometimes 4, and sometimes 5. Decisions that affect only one product, one customer group, or one geographic area keep the organization running in place. To grow faster than competitors, one must make decisions and investments that enhance the competitiveness of multiple products, multiple customers, and multiple geographic markets – *simultaneously!*

Importance Of Areas Of Excellence

Why are Areas of Excellence an integral part of *Strategic Thinking?* No company has the resources to develop skills equally in all areas. A company, therefore, has two key strategic decisions to make if it wishes to attain supremacy over its competitors.

First, it must determine which strategic area will give it strategic supremacy and be the Driving Force of its strategy. Second, it must decide what Areas of Excellence it must cultivate to enhance its supremacy. These Areas of Excellence should receive preferential treatment – fueled with more resources in order to develop a level of proficiency greater than any competitor. Once resources are diverted elsewhere, proficiency diminishes and the company loses its supremacy over its competitors.

Too often, organizations are distracted from what has made them successful. The most successful organizations are the ones in which the leader and senior management clearly understand their Driving Force and fuel the key Areas of Excellence required for success with more resources each year than they give to other areas. They then pursue their strategy with total dedication and without allowing any competitor to attain the same level of excellence in those few key capabilities. As Benjamin Disraeli so clearly noted many decades ago, "The secret to success is constancy of purpose." And, as Lewis Preston, the ex-CEO of J. P. Morgan, one of the world's most successful banks, said about the firm he headed: "We aren't likely to deviate radically from the clear strategic path we have been on since the days of the first Morgan partners."

Knowing what strategic area drives your organization and the Areas of Excellence required to support that strategy is essential to understanding which strategic weapon will give you a distinct and sustainable advantage in the marketplace. Our experience has clearly shown that any strategy can work, but that no company can pursue more than one strategy, each supported by two or three Areas of Excellence at any one moment in time.

CEO Interview

RASTERGRAPHICS

Rak Kumar
Chief Executive Officer
RasterGraphics

> **"The only way you can beat the bigger players
> is understanding the sandbox you're playing in
> and changing the game."**
>
> – *Rak Kumar*

Judo experts have always known that size doesn't matter. In fact, with the right strategy, small size can be used as an *advantage* as business competitors vie for supremacy. As this story illustrates, a smaller combatant may be able to use its agility and strategic focus as weapons so powerful that it can topple and defeat larger competitors.

An undaunted commitment to this principle enabled a small, specialized printer manufacturer to leverage its Driving Force and Areas of Excellence so effectively that it not only defeated two much larger competitors, but also ran them *completely out of business.* Says Rak Kumar, CEO of RasterGraphics, now part of Océ, "The only way you can beat the bigger players is by clearly understanding the sandbox you're playing in and changing the game in order to dominate that sandbox. You need to understand the whole concept of Driving Force and the one or two capabilities you must excel at – your Areas of Excellence – because you have limited resources and you need to know where to use those resources to strengthen these Areas of Excellence. That's the only way to win."

And win they have, as dedication to this simple credo enabled Kumar's company to grow from $25 million in sales to $130 million in four years, with 30 percent annual growth predicted going forward. This, despite the fact that they were playing in a sandbox dominated by much larger companies – divisions of Xerox and Lockheed – that dwarfed them in size.

Here's how it happened, as Kumar recounts this David and Goliath (actually David and Goliath and Goliath's bigger brother) tale.

"Back in 1996 we were a small company, called RasterGraphics, growing at about 25 percent a year. We make what we call printers for wide format imaging. That means we make printers for displays on the side of a bus or a Macy's window or a billboard," Kumar explains. "But when you have only about $25 million in revenue, you have limited resources, and we had very large companies as competitors. We were competing with Calcomp, a $400 million Lockheed division, and a division of Xerox that was at about $200 million at that time. Our big challenge was, as a small business with a good growth rate and good technology, what should we focus on? What should our strategy be over the next three to five years to continue to build the business at that rate and not get killed by giants like the Xeroxes and the Lockheeds of the world?"

To assist the management team in making these crucial decisions, they enlisted the help of DPI and its *Strategic Thinking Process.* The DPI approach appealed to them because of its participatory nature.

"We looked at all the traditional BCG-type models, and we felt that there are two approaches to developing strategy. One approach is getting outside people to *tell* you what to do. At the root of the *other* approach, as Mike Robert always says, is the concept that the people who know your business best are the people *on your own team* and that they should create their own strategy. So, working with DPI was really an attempt on our part to get some help, and get the whole team to sit down together and come up with a game plan that made sense for our size of company and the environment we're living in," says Kumar.

"We felt that the DPI process was excellent in the sense that it was really a process that forced us to answer our own questions. And since *we* know the industry, the issues and the challenges, we felt this was the best way for us to define our own strategy, one that we would own. When it's your people's own strategy, execution becomes that much easier because they developed it, they believe in it, and they have ownership of it. And it's been the same strategy since '96. We have not changed it in the slightest, even when we went through a very bad hiccup in 1998 because of a technology failure. A technology provided to us by one of our partners failed in the field. We went through a disaster, but we never took our eyes off the ball. To this day, the whole management team still feels that what kept us going was this *incredible focus* on that single sentence that DPI helped us develop called the Business Concept – *'Be the leader in wide format imaging systems and only that.'* We continue to live by that every day."

The process provided the forum that the company's management needed in order to get agreement on that concise Business Concept. In the course of the sessions it quickly became clear that the selection of a Driving Force and its related Areas of Excellence would be the platform from which their future would spring. As in most companies, there were, at the beginning of the sessions, a variety of opinions among the key players as to the right Driving Force.

Says Kumar, "Some people said we should be Customer Class-driven, a one-stop solutions provider. We should offer everything a customer needs – the printer, the software, the ink, the paper. Others said, 'Let's just stay focused on one area we know well and be Technology-driven.' Still others said, 'Let's just build printers' – a Product-driven strategy. We had always talked about these three components of the business without knowing that there is a way to look at them through a concept that DPI calls 'Driving Force.' Before we went through the process and began to sort out these things," says Kumar, "we had people who would say, 'Look, we sell to this customer, why don't we develop some complementary products and sell them at the same time.' The difficulty with this concept is that when you're small, with only $25 million in business, your marketing people can only focus on so many things. They really only have the resources to focus on your own products. We began to realize, through the logic of the process, that when they go out and say to the customer, 'Let me show you some paper,' or 'Let me show you some laminators,' or 'Let me show you some PCs,' we really don't add any value from these additional activities. They don't make us any stronger in our sandbox. In fact, they make us *weaker* because they dilute our limited resources. Also, we had to look at our technology, which is very good. Were we successful because we were a technology company? Or, were we successful because we understood the market the best?"

In order to fully envision the implications of each choice, the process enabled the work teams to create pictures of where each Driving Force might take the company in the future.

As Kumar explains, "We played out all three scenarios – Product, Technology, and User/Customer Class. It was very clear from the moment we began these discussions that a Customer Class Driving Force, for a $25 million company trying to fulfill all the needs of a commercial printer, was not a viable strategy. We came to the same conclusion regarding the Technology-driven strategy. We had a technology that had been successful only in a very small niche area, and we couldn't see how we could expand it into other applications. The discussion that really convinced us more than anything else was that over the previous six years, we had seen exceptional growth every time we launched a new wide format printer product. Then we'd get to a certain stage, and after a period of about six months we'd have a dry spell. We would then introduce the next product and we'd go through another dramatic surge. Everybody kind of looked at each other and said, 'Boy, this is so simple, isn't it.' We are so well known as a wide format printer *product* company. We just need to focus on the Area of Excellence called Product Development. The whole team must make sure that the product doesn't slip. We must do everything possible to nurture, support, and help the R&D team, make them part of the strategy process, and explain how critical they are for our business and our ability to compete with the Xeroxes and the Lockheeds.

"We concluded that if we did those things, we could be the best at Product Development. We could beat them because they move slowly, they're bigger companies, have other products to worry about, and have different Driving Forces than ours. Plus, they don't have our focus. So it became clear to everyone that we should be Product-driven. We make a specific category of wide format printers and that's it.

"Our strategy was simple, yet it gave enormous focus, and we have never deviated from that. We defined our Driving Force to be Product – 'wide format printers.' We then defined our Areas of Excellence as Product Development and Sales and Service. That focus allowed us to introduce a series of new printers at a pace that the other guys could not keep up with. It was that simple concept that has set us on the path to supremacy in our sandbox."

Like the judo expert, they proceeded to use their R&D expertise and agility to move faster than their larger competitors. They began to work their Critical Issues, nurturing the Product Development Area of Excellence, and developed a stream of innovative new products, supporting them with the most knowledgeable sales and marketing force in the sandbox.

Gradually, this absolute dedication to refining and enhancing these Areas of Excellence amplified their "supremacy gap" and took its toll on their competitors.

Incredibly, a couple of years later, both Xerox's and Lockheed's wide format printer divisions were *out of business*, in spite of healthy growth in demand for this particular class of printer.

"I believe these competitors, because they were so much bigger, first of all, couldn't focus on any one thing. Without as clear a concept as we created through the DPI process, we overtook them in Product Development and we never faced tough competition from that day forward because their products were always from the last generation of technology. In the end, they just gave up.

"One of them, Calcomp, in our view, wasn't clear on whether they were a Product company or a Technology company. They got into developing some futuristic technology and spent a hundred million dollars on R&D, but never commercialized it. Instead of staying focused on developing printers, they developed something like an integrated circuit, a chip that goes *into* the printer. It was that lack of focus – in my mind anyway – that finally destroyed their business.

"Xerox actually pulled out of the business completely," Kumar continues. "A $200 million division is gone. Calcomp Lockheed no longer exists either; it went bankrupt. So it is really very fulfilling to see that these huge corporations – with all their incredible resources and market presence, but without a focused, well articulated strategy – could fumble and just disappear," Kumar says.

8

How Strategic Product Innovation Breeds Supremacy

**"New-to-the-market products are
the fuel of corporate longevity."**

There was a time, not so long ago, that when you went to the national sales meeting, you were treated to a barrage of color slides shown through projectors made by Kodak or Bell and Howell. Then along came Microsoft's PowerPoint, for better or worse, and these ubiquitous projectors, and the slide-making equipment that went with them, were obsolete.

There was a time, not so long ago, that every desk in many offices had a Wang word processor, which promised a "paperless office." Then came the PC, and Wang nearly was out of business almost overnight.

There was a time, not so long ago, that Keds were the leading sneakers for kids. Then along came Nike and Reebok.

There was a time, not so long ago, when there was a Schwinn ten-speed bicycle, or two, in garages everywhere. Then along came Cannondale and Trek with high-tech bikes that ultimately forced Schwinn into bankruptcy.

There was time, not so long ago, that Telex machines were found in every office in the world. And there was a time, not so long ago, that there was a Singer sewing machine in every home in America and many other countries.

There was a time, not so long ago, when these companies and many more – such as Addressograph Multigraph, Friden, and Borden's – were powerhouses in their respective sandboxes with supremacy over all their competitors. However, just a few years later, their supremacy has disintegrated, together with their stock prices, and billions in shareholder value has been destroyed. What did these companies do, or not do, to descend from the ecstasy of supremacy to the footnotes of corporate history books?

Lack Of Strategic Product Innovation

The strategy of most companies is deployed through the introduction and commercialization of new products. Therefore, any company that wishes to perpetuate its supremacy over a long period of time needs to have in place an ongoing and aggressive *new product creation program.* Unfortunately, such was not the case in the companies mentioned above. Many other companies, which had ongoing new product development programs, could extend their supremacy over their competitors for very long periods of time – companies like Johnson & Johnson, Caterpillar, 3M, Mercedes, Sony, Honda, and Microsoft to name but a few.

New Products Are Not Always New Products

As noted in a previous chapter, the "profile" of a company is seen in the nature of the products the company offers, the nature of customers it makes these available to, the nature of the market segments that these customers reside in, and the nature of the geographic markets in which it operates.

If a CEO wishes to change the *profile* of the company, this is done by the creation and commercialization of *new* products. During our research into the subject of product innovation, we noticed that most companies concentrate their entire product innovation effort on incremental or marginal improvements to *existing products.* This type of product innovation is not strategic in nature since there is no attempt to change the "look" of the products the company offers.

In fact, while working with companies considered to be the best at product innovation, we discovered that even these companies had difficulty defining what a *new product* was. Thus, our first area of investigation was to identify the various categories of new product opportunities. Over time, we uncovered *five* categories of new product opportunities. These are:

New-to-the-Market. These are products that, when introduced, were unique to the market and the world. No similar products existed anywhere. Examples consist of 3M's Post-it® Notes and Sony's Walkman and VCR.

New-to-Us. When Panasonic introduced its own version of the VCR, it was not new-to-the-market since Sony had done it before, but it was new to Panasonic.

Product Extensions. In this category, we find two types: *incremental* and *quantum leap.* An example of an *incremental* extension is 3M's adaptation of the original Post-it® Notes into larger sizes, shapes, and colors. Boeing's announcement of a supersonic passenger jet is a *quantum leap* extension. The technology required is a significant step beyond producing its standard passenger jets.

New Customers. This category applies to the introduction of current products to new customers.

New Markets. This category applies to the introduction of current products to new market segments or new geographic areas.

The Em-phá-sis On The Wrong Syl-lá-ble

The next area we investigated was: In which category did they invest most of their resources? Guess what over two hundred companies answered. Right! *Product extensions* . . . of the *incremental* type. The food and packaged goods industries, for example, have perfected the art of "new and improved" products in different colors and sizes. Unfortunately, incremental extensions only bring *incremental revenues.* Only *new-to-the-market* products create new revenue streams. Most companies are putting their em-phá-sis on the wrong syl-lá-ble. In other words, they are pouring their money into the wrong type of product innovation.

The Four Deadly Sins That Kill Strategic Product Innovation

Since new-to-the-market products are the essence of strategic supremacy, we then set out to identify the obstacles that caused companies to spend almost all their time, money, and energy on product extensions at the expense of new-to-the-market products. Our discovery? Most companies committed one, or more, of four "sins" that killed new product creation and led to a company's loss of supremacy over its competitors. Unfortunately, all four were self-inflicted wounds.

Sin #1: Too Much Focus On Current Customers

Who do most books on product innovation tell you to consult in order to get inspiration for new products? The obvious answer: your customers. Wrong . . . dead wrong! If a company focuses its entire effort on current customers as a source for new products, it will always end up with *incremental* products. The reason is very simple. *Current* customers are very good at telling you what is *currently wrong* with your *current product.* They can do this well because they do side-by-side comparisons and they identify *performance gaps* in your product relative to your competitors. Naturally, you go back to the factory, tweak the product a little, and come back with an incremental improvement. And the pattern is set and keeps repeating itself.

Worse than that, your current customers can begin to

dominate your product development process. We often see this in working with clients. Borroughs Corporation, a company that makes, among other things, checkout lines for retail stores, had gradually gotten itself into this predicament. The company found itself responding to nearly every customer request for tweaks, refinements, and custom designs. Said CEO Tim Tyler who is interviewed in the following section of this book:

> "It was driving our inventories and engineering costs through the roof. I read an article in *Fortune* about Boeing and how they were faced with the problem of having seven or eight airplane frame models, yet they were offering something like thirty-three thousand different variations of galleys and bathrooms, and that was us to a 'T.' "

Borroughs used the *Strategic Product Innovation Process* we describe later in this chapter to analyze the problem and come up with a game-changing solution: a standardized product that meets all of its customers' essential needs, and is easily customizable to fit each customer's unique "look" – all at a very competitive cost. Customers readily embraced the concept and Borroughs's margins recovered nicely.

Current customers cannot be depended on for your new product ideas because they are *not* very competent at telling you what they will need *in the future.* Some examples:

Not one of 3M's millions of customers ever asked 3M for Post-it® Notes. Not one of Chrysler's millions of customers ever asked for a minivan. Not one of Sony's millions of customers ever asked Mr. Morita for a Walkman or a VCR. No one on this planet ever asked Steve Jobs and Steve Wozniak for an Apple computer. And the list goes on. These are all products that originated in the minds of the *creator, not the recipient.* There is a very good reason for this, as articulated by Akio Morita, the founder of Sony:

> "Our plan is to influence the public with new products instead of asking which products they want. The public doesn't know what is possible. We do."

Another person who said it as eloquently was the recently retired CEO of 3M, Livio DeSimone:

"The most interesting products are the ones that people need but can't articulate that they need."

In order to breed competitive supremacy and create new *revenue streams*, it is imperative to concentrate a company's product innovation resources on *new-to-the-market* products.

These are products that satisfy *future implicit needs* that you have identified and that your customers cannot articulate to you today. In this manner, the result will be products that will allow you to *change the game and perpetuate your supremacy.*

Sin #2: Protect The "Cash Cow" Mentality

Every company, over time, has products that become cash cows. *Never worship at the altar of the cash cow.* You will lose your supremacy. IBM is a case in point.

IBM's cash cow, as we all know, has been its mainframes – once the workhorses of the computing industry. In 1968, in its Swiss laboratories, IBM invented the first microchip – the RISC chip – with more processing capacity than its smaller mainframes. A small computer prototype, powered by this chip, was built and could have been the first PC the world would have seen. IBM, however, made a deliberate decision *not* to introduce that chip because it could foresee the devastation it might have on its mainframe business. In 1994, twenty-six years later and maybe twenty-six years too late, IBM finally introduced the RISC chip under the name PowerPC. In the meantime, IBM lost the opportunity to be the powerhouse in the *consumer* market that it is in the *business* market.

The same happened at Xerox. The company worshiped so diligently at the altar of large copiers that it did not see the advent of a stealth competitor – Canon – with small copiers. Furthermore, it failed to capitalize on unique inventions that were developed in its Silicon Valley laboratories, such as the "mouse" and inkjet printers, both used successfully by Apple later.

General Motors's fixation on large, gas-guzzling cars of questionable quality caused it to fail to foresee the entry of Toyota and Honda into the U.S. market with small, high-quality cars that have reduced GM to half the company it used to be.

Sin #3: The Mature Market Syndrome

"Our industry is mature. There is no more growth in these markets."

Many would claim that the reason products become generic, prices come down to the lowest levels, and growth stops is that the "market is mature." Mature markets, in our view, are a myth.

Consider some examples. Who would have thought fifteen years ago that people would pay three hundred dollars for a pair of shoes? Running shoes at that! After all, everyone had a pair of ten dollar sneakers and the market was mature. Then along came Nike and Reebok and the "mature market" exploded.

Who would have believed a few years ago that anyone would pay four dollars for a cup of coffee? Yet Starbucks has revolutionized the take-out coffee business by introducing unique products and marketing in a "mature" industry dominated by Dunkin' Donuts for decades. Dunkin' Donuts had mastered the perfect fifty-cent bottomless cup. A cup of coffee, after all, was just a cup of coffee.

Who would have thought fifteen years ago that people would pay five thousand dollars for a bicycle? After all, everyone had a hundred dollar bicycle and the market was mature. Then along came Shimano, Cannondale, Trek, and others with 18- and 21-speed bicycles and a new type of bike called a "mountain bike," and the "mature market" exploded.

Two CEOs who have based their success on debunking the notion of "mature" markets are Jack Welch, General Electric's famous ex-CEO, and Lawrence Bossidy, formerly CEO of AlliedSignal. Jack Welch preaches, "Mature markets are a state of mind," while Bossidy says, "There is no such thing as a mature market. What we need are *mature executives* who can make markets grow."

Sin #4: The Commodity Product Fallacy

"We're in the commodity business" is another mindset that can bring down a company's supremacy. This is also a state of mind. Products become commodities when management *convinces* itself that they are. It's a self-fulfilling prophecy.

An example is baking soda, a "commodity" product that has been around since the days of the Pharaohs – until someone placed a small quantity in a refrigerator and noticed that it absorbed odors. Not long after came baking soda deodorant, followed by baking soda toothpaste, and recently, baking soda diapers.

Frank Perdue pioneered the concept of branding chicken, promising more tender, better tasting chicken. Before Perdue, chicken was chicken, and the only price factors were supply and demand.

Then there is the "mother" of all commodities – water. Yet look at what the French can do with water. They have mastered the marketing of this mundane commodity by branding it under a variety of names, such as Vitel, Evian, and Perrier. Knowing that people are becoming more concerned about the quality of the water they drink, they began to market *bottled* water at exorbitant prices. This concept was immediately successful, even in places where tap water is excellent and essentially free. Through brilliant marketing, they made water "trendy," creating "designer brands," and charged even more.

Beverage manufacturers are now taking the concept a big step further – adding *nutrients* to water to create a new category – *sports* water. One of these even incorporates the "grandmother" of all commodities – *oxygen*!

New-To-The-Market Products Breed Supremacy

Sony, 3M, Canon, Microsoft, Johnson & Johnson, Caterpillar, Schwab, and many others maintain their control of the sandbox, not by introducing "me-too" products but, rather, by focusing their resources on the creation of new-to-the-market products that have three inherent characteristics which contribute to breeding supremacy over their competitors:

- A period of *exclusivity*. When you are the only product in the market, you are the *only one.*

- During this period of exclusivity, you can obtain *premium prices* as opposed to me-too products where every transaction comes down to haggling over price.

- Being first to the market allows you to build in barriers that make it very difficult for competitors to gain entry into your game.

After all, that's what supremacy is all about: changing the game and creating the rules that competitors wishing to play your game must submit to.

The Strategic Product Innovation Process

Strategic supremacy is highly dependent on the organization's ability to create and bring to market new products more often and more quickly than its competitors. We view new product creation as the *fuel of corporate longevity* – 3M, Johnson & Johnson, and Sony introduce hundreds of new products every year. The secret of these product innovator superstars is a deliberate process that causes product innovation. This systematic process is known and used by everyone in the company.

Observing this phenomenon, we at DPI went on to *codify* this process being practiced *implicitly* at these kinds of companies. The result is a unique process called *Strategic Product Innovation*, which makes new product creation a learnable, *repeatable* process. This process can be used by an organization to create and commercialize new-to-the-market products (not seen before) that leverage the company's Driving Force and Areas of Excellence, and generate new revenue streams, allowing the company to grow faster than its competitors.

This conscious, repeatable business practice consists of the following four steps.

Creation. Carefully monitor the ten sources in your business environment, listed on the following page, from which you can create a broad range of opportunities for new-to-the-market products.

Assessment. Measure the new product opportunities in terms of costs, benefits, strategic fit, and difficulty of implementation. These criteria will let you know which opportunities should be pursued further – and which should be abandoned.

Development. Once a commitment is made, try to anticipate the critical factors that will cause the new product to succeed or fail in the marketplace.

Pursuit. Develop a specific implementation plan that promotes success and avoids failure.

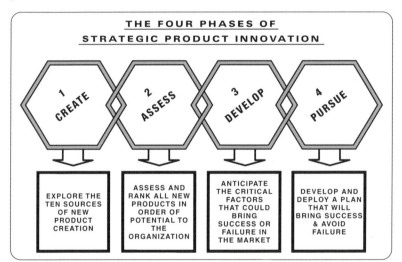

THE FOUR PHASES OF STRATEGIC PRODUCT INNOVATION

1 CREATE	2 ASSESS	3 DEVELOP	4 PURSUE
EXPLORE THE TEN SOURCES OF NEW PRODUCT CREATION	ASSESS AND RANK ALL NEW PRODUCTS IN ORDER OF POTENTIAL TO THE ORGANIZATION	ANTICIPATE THE CRITICAL FACTORS THAT COULD BRING SUCCESS OR FAILURE IN THE MARKET	DEVELOP AND DEPLOY A PLAN THAT WILL BRING SUCCESS & AVOID FAILURE

The Creation Step

Our research in this area of corporate endeavor has uncovered ten sources from which new-to-the-market product concepts can emerge. These consist of:

- Unexpected successes

- Unexpected failures

- Unexpected external events

- Process weaknesses

- Industry/structural changes

- High growth areas

- Converging technologies

- Demographic shifts

- Perception shifts

- New knowledge

Some examples of each follow.

Unexpected Successes

McDonald's unbelievable growth since the 1960s began with Ray Kroc's curiosity about why he was selling so many milk-shake machines to a small hamburger stand owned by the McDonald brothers. By examining the cause of an unexpected success, as Kroc did, we are able to uncover opportunities to create new-to-the-market products.

Even though Steve Jobs and Bill Gates may claim differently, I am convinced that neither expected their first products – the Apple PC and Microsoft's original PC software respectively – to be as successful as they proved to be or that they would lead to an entire new universe of new-to-the-market products. Bill Gates even offered that software to IBM for $75,000 but IBM refused, which, in hindsight, has probably been IBM's biggest strategic mistake.

Unexpected Failures

Failures, large and small, happen every day. They are generally viewed negatively, yet in many of them are the seeds of success. The failure of the Edsel, for example, led to the development of the highly successful, and game-changing, Mustang.

Unexpected External Events

The world throws unexpected curve balls at us all the time. Two such events – the Asian financial crisis and a sudden decline in IT growth – threatened the previously very successful strategy of DPI client Teckwah, a Singapore-based commercial printer. These changes caused management to rethink the future, particularly since the IT industry was their primary market. Teckwah decided to provide a range of printing-related services that no other printer offered. This rethinking of their strategy and the offering of these new "products" evolved into a very successful new business model – supply chain management – and expanded Teckwah's market scope, enabling future expansion into new segments, such as pharmaceuticals.

Process Weaknesses

FedEx was created to exploit a major weakness in the U.S. Postal Service – its inability to deliver all the mail within twenty-four hours. If the Postal Service ever corrected that weakness, it would be the death of FedEx.

One of our clients mentioned earlier, Roberts Express, exploited a process weakness in JIT deliveries to the auto industry to create a game-changing service in the trucking business. It was so successful that none other than FedEx decided to make Roberts part of their business.

Industry/Structural Changes

Changes such as the deregulation and internationalization of many businesses have led to new product and service concepts. These changes have given rise to companies such as MCI, Sprint, alternative local telephone carriers, electric power resellers, satellite dishes, and peripheral products like decoders.

High Growth Areas

The stupendous growth and penetration of PCs over the past decade created nearly endless opportunities for innovative *software* for business and entertainment uses. This continues despite leveling off of demand for PCs. Have you noticed unusual growth in an area of your business or *somebody else's* that might create an opportunity for you?

Converging Technologies

A lot has been said in the media about the convergence of computer and telecom technologies. Many of the predictions have come to pass with a wave of various personal communications devices. Much less has been said, however, about the convergence of electronics and biotechnology – a scientific trend that began with the now archaic-looking Jarvik heart. The pacemaker and other similar devices are products that emerged from this incipient branch of science. Much more sophisticated advances are just on the horizon. One surprising player in this relatively new field is Motorola, which is developing products for use in applications as diverse as bioinformatics, molecular and cell biology, and genetics. That's a long way from cell phones. The situation is somewhat unique in that both electronic information processing and biotechnology are sciences in which new knowledge is emerging at an accelerating rate, opening an unprecedented range of new product and market opportunities.

Demographic Changes

The aging of the Baby Boom generation has given rise to a wide assortment of new products. One of the most profitable is the "New Age Beverage" category championed by startups like SoBe. Knowing that the Boomer generation is struggling to hang onto youth and vitality, SoBe mixed various strange-sounding herbs with water and flavors, enticing the consumer with promises of greater physical and mental well-being. So successful was SoBe, in a market assumed to be controlled by the distribution networks of Coke and Pepsi, that Pepsi recently acquired a controlling interest in the former cottage business for just under $400 million after a heated bidding battle with none other than Coca-Cola.

Perception Change

One of the twentieth century's most enduring brands – Oldsmobile – fell prey to this type of change. Once a symbol of stature and upper-middle class solidity, the perception of Olds gradually came to symbolize "old, stodgy, and boring" to younger consumers. Realizing this, apparently too late, GM tried to reposition Olds under the slogan "Not Your Father's Oldsmobile." It didn't stick, and the division flailed about looking for a way to revive its popularity until its demise was finally announced in 2001. Meanwhile, Toyota is *leveraging* the same type of changes in perception about cars – they have to be "cool" to appeal to a youthful driver – to create a new product line called Matrix with its own "youth-friendly" areas at dealerships, catering to some of the same consumers that Oldsmobile failed to attract.

New Knowledge

The latest new knowledge, which holds immense implications for future products, is the mapping of the human genome. This remarkable advance promises to open far-reaching new avenues of treatment for a wide variety of diseases. New knowledge concerning the effects of nutrition on human health is creating the opportunity for a wide variety of new products called wellness foods, nutraceuticals, and medical foods.

Opportunity's Constant Knock

Although many executives tell us, before they use our process, that there are no new product opportunities for their companies, we have never found that to be true. The problem is not that opportunity knocks but once, but that it is knocking every day in the multitude of changes facing organizations. We have found – initially to our surprise, and always to the surprise of clients – that organizations have a surplus of opportunities. They just don't know where to look for these in a systematic manner. One of our clients generated over twelve hundred, and another over four hundred, new-to-the-market product ideas in businesses that thought themselves to be in commodity, low price, low margin, mature market industries.

By exploring each of these ten sources and their derivatives, management can generate dozens, if not hundreds, of new-to-the-market products. Once in the "hopper," the real challenge for management is to discriminate among these in order to select those that promise the most potential within the company's strategy.

The Assessment Step

The second step consists of ranking all these new product concepts in terms of their potential for the company. This is done by anticipating the relationship between:

- Cost
- Benefit
- Strategic fit
- Ease/difficulty of commercialization

Judging all concepts on these criteria allows management to rank them in order of attractiveness to the organization. Some of the new concepts with lesser potential are abandoned after this step.

Cost-Benefit Relationship

The first two criteria are obvious enough – *cost and benefit.* Each opportunity needs to be assessed in terms of its relative cost versus relative benefit.

Anyone engaged in product creation and introduction should want to know fairly concisely and rapidly the cost and benefit of implementing this opportunity. Two of the generic questions usually asked are:

- What is the cost of implementing this new product or market opportunity?
- What is the benefit of implementing this new product or market opportunity?

The following is a checklist of considerations that contribute either to the potential cost or potential benefit of an opportunity. An evaluation of each will allow you to create a framework within which the cost-benefit relationship can be clarified and scrutinized.

Checklist: Cost/Benefit

Cost	**Benefit**
❏ People	❏ Market share
❏ Materials	❏ Return/Profit
❏ Equipment	❏ Prestige/Image
❏ Research	❏ Service/Satisfaction
❏ Marketing	❏ Earnings/Dividends
❏ Legal	❏ Fallout/Residuals
❏ Promotion	❏ Safety/Security
❏ Time	❏ Quality
❏ Pilot	❏ Morale/Motivation
❏ Contingency	❏ Growth/Size

Strategic Fit/Difficulty Of Implementation Relationship

The next two assessment criteria are less obvious – *strategic fit* and *difficulty of implementation*. These two criteria are probably more important than the cost-benefit ratio, but unfortunately they are almost always overlooked.

Strategic Fit. How well does this new product or market opportunity fit the strategy of the business? This is a key question that is often not asked but always should be. Experience has shown that organizations that try to innovate *outside the strategic framework* of the business usually do not succeed.

By strategic fit, we mean the degree to which an opportunity fits a company's direction. The opportunity need not fit exactly at first, provided that it promises to fit well in the near future. So the issue concerns not just today's strategy but also the direction that the company is pursuing.

When an opportunity is pursued irrespective of strategic

thrust, the results are usually disappointing or even damaging. Several years ago, Exxon decided to enter the office information business and began an operation known as QXT. Despite the infusion of massive amounts of money and the work of some highly talented people, QXT was a disaster, and Exxon eventually dissolved it. The office products market simply was not a part of Exxon's direction and strategy as a company. That is, it could not be *made* a part of the nature and direction – the fabric – of Exxon's business. Consequently, it was doomed to failure from the start. A senior executive of Exxon recently told us that Exxon executives did not understand the office equipment business as well as they did the "trivia of the oil business," and so they could not manage or even judge the opportunities of the former. There was *no strategic fit.*

New product or new market creation is not a question of unbridled enthusiasm spinning off into every direction of the compass at once. It is a question of organized, purposeful, and *focused* attempts to create new products that fit the organization's *business goals.* Consequently, new product innovation must be undertaken within the purview of corporate strategy and its *future strategic profile.*

Assessing Strategic Fit. If the Driving Force of a company is not entirely clear (the company hasn't used the *Strategic Thinking Process*), we can still assess strategic fit by asking the following questions.

Questions: Strategic Fit

- How similar are the products this opportunity brings compared to the products we currently offer?

- How similar are the markets (segments or geographic) this opportunity brings compared to the markets we currently serve?

- How similar are the customers this opportunity brings compared to the customers we currently serve?

- How similar are the production capabilities and/or processes this opportunity brings compared to the production capabilities we currently have?

- How similar is the technology this opportunity needs compared to the technology we currently know?

- How similar are the sales/marketing methods this opportunity requires compared to the ones we currently use?

- How similar are the distribution/delivery methods this opportunity requires compared to the ones we currently use?

- How similar are the human resources and skills this opportunity requires compared to those we have currently?

- How will the size/growth and return/profit criteria compare to our current levels of achievement?

The more similarity there is in each of the above areas, the closer the strategic fit. The more dissimilar they are, the more remote the fit will be – unless, of course, the discrepancy is that the opportunity represents higher size/growth or return/profit potential than the company is accustomed to. We have found that better than "normal" financial expectations are more often the rule than the exception simply because the new products often represent a change from me-too commodities to unique, differentiated products.

Difficulty Of Implementation. The fourth criterion is *difficulty of implementation*. Again, we have seen many good opportunities fail because management had simply understated the degree of difficulty in trying to capitalize on an opportunity.

The relative ease or difficulty of implementation really refers to the "organizational immune system" that every company seems to possess. We've seen numerous cases of good ideas that presented high benefit at reasonable cost within the organization's strategic framework, but were rejected by this immune system.

A case in point was Honda's marketing of its Acura automobiles when they were first introduced. These cars represented Honda's entry into the luxury auto marketplace. Honda made a decision at the outset that these luxury cars could not be sold through the same dealerships that were handling the rest of the Honda line. It was apparently felt that the Honda "sales culture" would not be conducive to selling these high-end automobiles. So Honda's decision was to market these new cars only in separate dealerships, and even then, only in those dealerships that maintained a certain physical distance from any nearby Honda dealerships. This decision was taken even at the risk of offending current Honda dealers. Honda clearly believed that its *organizational immune system* was not ready for the luxury auto.

Even IBM, with all its success in the mainframe business, had some initial difficulties when it entered the PC field. The reasons were obvious. The customer base was not the same. Mainframes were sold to companies, PCs to individuals. Thus, the selling and distribution methods were different, and IBM had no experience selling directly to consumers.

The degree of difficulty encountered in introducing new products or entering new markets is directly proportionate to the number of changes that the organization will need to make from its current modus operandi. The more changes, the greater the degree of difficulty; the fewer changes, the less difficulty.

To assess the degree of implementation difficulty, the following question needs to be asked: *How much change will be required in each of the following areas to implement this new product or market opportunity?*

Checklist: Implementation Difficulty

❑ Organization Structure

❑ Processes and/or Systems

❑ Skills and/or Talents

❏ Manufacturing Methods and Capabilities

❏ Selling and/or Marketing Methods

❏ Distribution or Delivery Methods

❏ Technologies

❏ Capital and Financing

❏ Legal and Regulatory Issues

❏ Image, Reputation, and Quality

❏ Compensation Systems

❏ Raw Materials

❏ Customer Services

❏ Corporate Culture

Once the changes have been identified, the element that will determine the degree of difficulty is the amount of control the implementors have over those changes. The more control, the less difficulty; the less control, the more difficulty. Another key question then is: *How much control do we have over each of the changes we will need to make in our current modus operandi to implement this new product?*

By assessing each new product on the basis of these four criteria, we can rank them in terms of their overall potential for the company. And, like milk and cream, the best new product opportunities rise to the top of the list and the balance are discarded or saved for future reworking.

The Pursuit Step

New product introductions succeed or fail based on management's ability to anticipate the *critical factors* that will deliver one or the other result. The development step is the *transition* to the formal pursuit, or introduction, of the new opportunity. It is the organization's ability to *think* through the implementation *beforehand*.

Best-Case And Worst-Case Scenarios. The first part of the pursuit step is to construct scenarios. In other words, management must try to foresee what would be the best possible set of outcomes as well as the worst possible set of outcomes for each new product opportunity. These scenarios can be captured in the following format.

Each new product, starting with the best one first, is now examined, and best- and worst-case scenarios are constructed using the results we might expect if we were to pursue this opportunity. The following are the questions to ask.

Process Questions:

- **Best-case scenario:** If we pursued this opportunity, what are all the best results this opportunity would bring?

- **Worst-case scenario:** If we pursued this opportunity, what are all the worst results this opportunity would bring?

The second part of the pursuit step is to start *thinking* about how we can achieve the best-case scenario while avoiding the worst-case scenario. In order to do this, we must now attempt to identify the *critical factors* that will lead to one or the other of the two scenarios. The following are questions to ask about critical factors.

Process Questions:

- What critical factors will cause the worst-case scenario?

- What critical factors will cause the best-case scenario?

Having listed the outcomes that would produce the worst-case and best-case scenarios, you're now in a position to list the critical factors that will tend to bring about the best case, as well as the critical factors that will tend to bring about the worst case.

After the identification of all the critical factors of success or failure is completed, we are ready to proceed into the last, and final, step of new product or new market innovation – the launch.

The next step takes us from *transitional thinking* into the world of *implementation*. For new product and/or market concepts to be successful, the implementors must concentrate on two key elements. One is containing or *preventing* the worst-case scenario from materializing, and the other is assuring or *promoting* the best-case scenario. Thus, the need at this stage in the process is to introduce the concepts of *preventive* and *promotive* actions.

Preventive And Promotive Actions

The pursuit step concentrates on taking special actions to remove obstacles to the effective implementation of the opportunity. The fundamental premise is to now think of specific actions that will *prevent* the critical factors that would cause the worst-case scenario, while also thinking about actions to *promote* the critical factors that will cause the best possible outcome. Promotive actions seek to maximize the benefits of a new product, while preventive actions seek to mitigate the effects of the potential problems that might be encountered.

Building The Implementation Plan

Pursuit is the process of formulating an implementation plan and then beginning the actual implementation of opportunities. It relies heavily on the critical factors that were raised in the development step. It is a step that is specifically designed to focus on individual opportunities and bridge the gap between the *conceptualization* and the *actualization* of these opportunities. It allows you to analyze those factors that will determine success or failure for your opportunity and to assign *specific* actions that will help to enhance success and avoid failure. Pursuit is begun "on paper" before energy, resources, and reputations have been committed. Once the plan takes a coherent shape, implementation begins. Although the pursuit is not an absolute guarantee of success, it does function as an insurance policy – one designed to provide the greatest protection for you and your plan.

Strategy And Product Innovation At FLEXcon

A company with whom DPI has had a long-term relationship dating back to 1985 is FLEXcon, based in Spencer, Massachusetts. The company is a world leader in the manufacturing of laminated substrates and adhesives for a wide variety of applications across many industries. Here is what CEO Neil McDonough says about DPI's SPI process and its link to strategic focus:

> "New products are the lifeblood of our company. We put DPI's *Strategic Product Innovation Process* into place about eighteen months ago. And after eighteen months *30 percent of our sales come from new products.* We started with a goal of 30 percent in three years. Obviously, we blew that away. Through the first four months of this year, we came up with 179 products, using combinations of materials we had never made before. We made *and sold them.* So this has been very successful for us!

> "It all comes down to getting agreement on the Driving Force, and the Business Concept, so that you can develop the Critical Issues from there. It's very straightforward. You've just got to invest the time and do it. And do it with a facilitator who has the experience to force you through these questions and keep the process on track. Then, once you've gotten down to the Critical Issues, give people the tools to make the right decisions and get things done. If you're going to tackle complex issues, you've got to embed these concepts in your company's culture."

CEO Interview

Tim Tyler
President & Chief Executive Officer
Borroughs Corporation

**"Within the industry there is a lot of carnage
going on around us right now.
Our business is at an all time high."**

– Tim Tyler

If you've been in a big retail store or an industrial warehouse, you've seen Borroughs's products – automated checkout lines and special-purpose shelving. The trick in these markets is to somehow differentiate your offerings from the many "me-too" products in the marketplace while controlling design and production costs – essential concepts if you hope to pump up margins *and* grow the top line. The temptation is to let the *customer* dictate your product's design – leading to "me-too" products, since everyone's competing for the same customer, or to expensive over-customization for every customer that demands it.

142

This is the challenge Borroughs faced, particularly in its checkout line business. Despite a leadership position in the business and a customer list that contains the biggest names in retail, margins were dismal – victimized by rising engineering and manufacturing costs. It seemed that every customer – large and small – insisted on extensive customization of the product. And, following the established "rules" in their industry, they did it. After all, you can't say "no" to a customer.

Tim Tyler, President and CEO of the $50 million Michigan-based company, describes the situation this way: "One of the issues that we were having with the retail product line was that it is one of the most fickle industries you can imagine because all these chains of stores all want their own design, their own look. The majority of these companies, such as food retailers, are huge outfits. Most of them are multi-billion dollar organizations. They have severe problems with ergonomic workplace issues, and they all have their own ergonomic teams looking at how people work. The front end of a store is one of the largest overhead pieces of any of these operations."

In addition to endless variations on ergonomics, customers also want a distinctive design and look based on the individual cosmetic and functional requirements. For very large customers, engineering and production costs could be built into the volume price, but the further down the volume ladder they went, the less profitable these projects became.

Says Tyler, "For a long time, we had told the sales force, 'Go get business, bring it in here.' But then we would get some business from what we call the ma-and-pa stores, the guy that wants ten to fifteen lanes, and wants all these little nuances to it. So here we are, burdening our engineering department with all of this additional work – to go to the design shop, to program machines, to make product – and we'd always end up with additional inventory. It was driving our inventories and our engineering costs through the roof. I read an article in *Fortune* about Boeing and how they were faced with the problem of having about seven or eight airplane frame models, yet they were offering something like thirty-three thousand different variations of galleys and bathrooms, and that was us to a 'T'."

At the same time, the shelving product lines had problems of their own – little differentiation from rival products and a lot of price competition. Something had to be done to break these entrenched cycles.

Tyler and his management team decided to seek help in the form of DPI's dual processes – *Strategic Thinking* and *Strategic Product Innovation* – the former to create an overall strategy, the latter to organize and drive new product development.

Not surprisingly, they discovered through the *Strategic Thinking Process* that Borroughs is Product-driven – shelving and conveyorized equipment for retail and industrial customers. Additionally, they came to the realization that Product Development and Service were Areas of Excellence they would need to nurture continuously. Moreover, they realized in going through the process that they could break the mold in their industry, creating innovative new ways to disrupt the established rules that had limited their growth and profitability.

"We had about twenty-eight people that were involved in these processes. We had our marketing folks, outside sales people, a lot of engineers, and the senior management in the company. We worked hard at this thing, and it was very good. It helped us get everybody pointed in the right direction. You know, here is what we know we're good at, there's the product lines that we've got, and we're going to bear down on them and we're going to create new products and add value to our product every which way we can with the resources that we've got," says Tyler.

"DPI helped us define the way we would go about looking at these new product lines, and what we thought we could now bring to the marketplace, and we've been knocking these new product ideas down one at a time. Our process for developing new products is much more streamlined. And another thing that came out of it was that it established the process and the chain of command that we were going to use to bring these products to market. Our group bought into how this process would work and how we could use it as a strategic tool."

Changing The Game

"One of the things the DPI Partner, Mark Thompson, kept saying to us is, 'You need to look at changing the rules in your sandbox,' which has become a phrase I hear our people around here saying all the time now," Tyler states.

And change the rules they did in ways that have since greatly increased both top and bottom lines. On the checkout line side, for example, they have developed a game-changing solution – standardized checkout lines that can be easily customized – that provides the customer with the best product at a highly favorable price, while boosting Borroughs's margins up to new highs.

As Tyler explains, "The biggest thing in changing the rules with the retail line was that the DPI process really helped us identify where our opportunities were, what our strengths are, what our opportunities would be, and what to capitalize on. We came up with the idea that we could use our knowledge of all of the needs of our checkout line customers to develop a standardized product that wouldn't need constant re-engineering. Because we're in Michigan we have a lot of people who've come out of the automotive industry, including myself. We understand about having a platform and building off of that, and that is one of the things that DPI helped us with.

"We have since told our customers, 'Look, we've been making these checkout lanes probably longer than anyone else in the country. And we've been listening to you and applying all that experience to come up with a better way to provide what you want.' We're saying we have defined all of the basic needs. We can give them everything they want – we've studied the ergonomics and incorporated the latest thinking into a much more standardized product. We'll paint them any color, put any molding on them, and so on. And we can give them a product that is absolutely first quality at an extremely competitive price."

Meanwhile, most of Borroughs's competitors continue to go after highly customized, short-run business.

"We see a lot of our competitors doing exactly that. They're fine competitors, and that's the route they've chosen. But where we're different is that we're geared for volume, high production runs. That's where we can be very successful and that is really one of our great strengths," Tyler states.

"And to make sure we reach the profitability we want consistently, Mark Thompson helped us identify a filter that we would look at to be able to set margin targets and quantity targets. If we see potential products that don't pass the filter, we now say, 'If you can't make money at it, why do it?' That has helped us raise our margins substantially. And again, having all the people we had involved in the process, everybody understands what we're driving towards. I just had one of our sales managers in my office this morning and he was showing me a breakdown of a job we're quoting and he had it all – all the run sizes costed out, the discounts, and the discounts as they applied to what margins we might get off of it. He had our margin target circled. And he said, 'This is where we're at if we're trying to maintain our margin target to budget.' We now have a minimum budgeted margin target when we put our budgets together every year. We keep pushing it to a higher number, and we are being successful at it. This has become one of our stretch goals and one that our sales department loves to chase after."

Similar results have been achieved in the shelving line through creation of new products. One new product is a folding shelf unit to be offered to *consumers* – a new market for Borroughs. Another is a modular drawer system for automotive dealers and other markets with parts storage needs – a product that had been looked at as a commodity.

As Tyler explains, "With our modular drawers we completely took the high road. There are a lot of people that make this product and we viewed it as a product that will be in our industrial line for a long, long time, and that will service some big markets. So we decided we were going to design something that was better than everybody else's and at a more competitive price, and I believe we have done that. We have won a number of jobs where we've had our customers tell us that our quality was hands down better than the other people they've looked at."

Additionally, Borroughs has launched a focused technical service group to support industrial material handling system integrators that netted six million dollars in sales in the first year. They've also succeeded in resurrecting a product line that was in danger of being axed because of poor profitability. Analysis through the DPI process revealed a way to save the product and raise the margin by 10 percent.

"We analyzed who we were selling it to. We realized we were letting the customers dictate how we would make and price the product. Finally we just said, 'Enough is enough. We're not going to do that.' And the surprising thing was, when we raised the prices in that product line and told everyone this was happening, we didn't lose one customer. Now we have reached the point where there are some customers we have chosen to part company with due to low volume and profitability issues. We are direct in telling them that we do not feel as if we can be successful for them," says Tyler.

Borroughs has gotten religion about new product development but, more importantly, about applying the Strategic Filter they have all agreed upon.

"I can't emphasize enough what this process has done for us as a company, with us as a group looking at these things. The real driver has been that this has really defined how seriously everybody takes the filter. We examine each opportunity based on that. There is not a day that goes by that we don't have somebody from outside sales requesting something that is either driven by an end user customer or one of our distributor dealers and is outside our plan. And they'll ask the question, 'Well, how come you can't do that? That's what you used to do.' It's interesting because now when that happens there's a huddle that takes place amongst our managers and the people that have been involved with this process and everyone says, 'That's not what we agreed to. That's not how this thing works.'

"If you knew our Vice President of Operations, he's physically an imposing guy, he stomps his foot and says, 'That's not what we agreed to do.' It circulates right back through the organization and we give a diplomatic answer to the end user. What comes out of that is an alternative that we could provide him with and the reasons we think that it's a better idea. And again, we've been very successful in that approach.

"Within the industry there is a lot of carnage going on around us right now. I mean a lot of layoffs, that kind of thing. *Our* business is at an all time high, and I attribute a lot of that toward what we did with DPI's *Strategic Thinking* and *Strategic Product Innovation Processes*," says Tyler.

9

Supremacy Models That Will Change the Game

"Wars are won in the planning room, not on the battlefield."

– General Dwight Eisenhower

For the last year or so, we have been using our *Strategic Thinking Supremacy Process* that we started developing a few years ago with a number of clients. This has allowed us to validate our concepts and prove that they work in the "real world." Only *after* the concepts and the process had been validated did we write this book.

The overall objective of this process is to enable a company to develop a new strategy and business model that will *change the game to its advantage and strive for supremacy in its chosen sandbox.*

One part of our process calls for the formation of a "stealth" competitor" team whose mandate is to develop a "stealth" strategy and business model that would result in supremacy over all competitors in the sandbox of the future. The full mandate given to this team is:

- That the "stealth" competitor needs to be an organization that is not currently on our "radar screen" but will be interested in the Business Arena we will be part of in the future

- That the intent is nothing less than supremacy of the sandbox

- That the strategy and business model must be one that can actually be deployed by some company, if not your own

The following are examples from five of our clients. Each of these "stealth" strategies represents a dramatic departure from their current strategy. They also are strategies that will allow these companies to break "out of the box," rid themselves of "me-too" strategies, *differentiate* themselves from their competitors, and substantially increase the probability of asserting supremacy in their respective sandboxes.

The HVAC.com Strategy

There is a market out there known as the HVAC market. HVAC stands for "heating, ventilation, and air conditioning." In this market, or sandbox, there are a number of companies that supply equipment and products such as boilers, furnaces, air conditioners, floorboard heating panels, and ceiling ducts.

There are approximately two dozen players in the sandbox. Among them is our client who offers a wide variety of such products. The game in this sandbox is currently played according to the following rules:

- Most manufacturers work through reps.

- Most manufacturers have a love/hate relationship with their reps.

- All manufacturers interact with a number of parties, such as developers, contractors, builders, and architects, and there are a number of contacts with each before obtaining an order.

- All attempt to get "spec'd in" the customer's blueprint, which guarantees a long relationship with that customer.

- All work on the same price structure with the same volume and trade discounts.

- All work through third party installers.

- All manufacturers have very little name recognition with the end user and, frequently, even within the industry.

- The industry is highly fragmented.

During the *Strategic Thinking Supremacy* sessions with us, a "stealth" team was formed and given the mandate to develop a strategy that would reign supreme in the sandbox of the future. Looking at the Future Business Arena that the group had developed that morning, they decided that one of the major impediments to the conduct of business in this sandbox is that there are too many parties with which a manufacturer needs to interact. All these contacts slow the flow and often negatively affect the accuracy of the information needed to consummate a transaction. The team felt that a company that could reduce the number of players and streamline the information flow would achieve supremacy in the future sandbox.

The concept? HVAC.com. This company would be the hub for all players in the sandbox and the game would be changed in the following manner.

- HVAC.com would join the best manufacturers of different equipment into a network of "premier" suppliers to the HVAC sandbox.

- On the other side, this new entity would attempt to have the buyers – contractors, architects, developers – join a "private" club for customers of HVAC products.

- As a premier manufacturer, a company would receive "privileged" information from HVAC.com that would keep them abreast of what's going on in the sandbox. This would include information about upcoming construction projects, the names of the developer and contractor, and the mechanics of the bid process (who the competitors are likely to be, etc.).

- Members of the private customer club would also receive "privileged" information, such as advance notice on new products, changes in standards and codes, and group discounts if you purchased all your products from HVAC.com members.

How would all this happen and how would the flow of information be streamlined? The answer: the Internet. Here are the two models. The graphics throughout this chapter are rough representations created by these clients to help them to visualize these new models.

Current Model

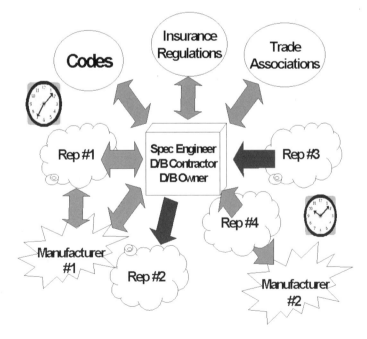

New Model

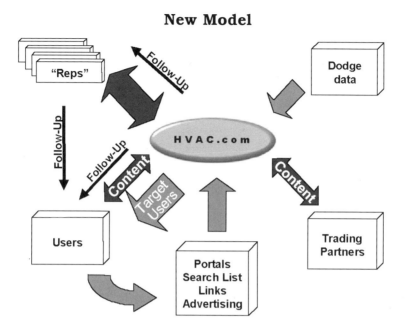

Food Shopping As It Will Be

Food retailing has probably been around since man has been on this planet and the game has not changed much over that period of time. It started with farmers bringing their produce to the open markets in nearby cities and displaying their produce on stands the best way they could in order to attract as many customers as possible. About the only major change that has occurred over the centuries is that these markets are now indoors, instead of outdoors. In today's indoor supermarket sandbox, the game is played in this manner:

- Build a store with 50,000 to 75,000 square feet of space.

- Locate these stores in densely populated areas in metropolitan cities and suburbs.

- Install row upon row of display shelves separated by aisles that you expect the customers to follow, all going in the same direction at the same time.

- Stock the shelves with large quantities of perishable and non-perishable goods that you hope will be purchased rapidly since the cost of keeping these in inventory is very high.

- Build end-of-aisle merchandising displays with discounted prices good only for a limited time.

- Use coupons and other promotional techniques to attract potential customers.

- Build a "chain" of these stores to develop brand name recognition and benefit from economies of scale.

Every retailer, including our client, operates this way and no one has supremacy. In fact, the CEO of this company opened the work session with the following introduction:

"Although we are operationally competent and, as a result, have been reasonably successful over the years, our position in the marketplace has not changed in the last thirty-two years. The reason is that all the competitors in our sandbox are cloning each other and no one gains at the others' expense. In the last few years, we've come to realize that we must have a distinctive strategy that will set us apart from these competitors so that we can enhance our market position.

"Since then, we have been searching for assistance but had not found anything satisfactory until we encountered DPI. Their process of *Strategic Thinking* and the concept of a "stealth" competitor intrigued us, and thus the reason we are here today. We must change our strategy and do something different or else our future will be no better than our past and that is not acceptable.

"Our strategy is equal to that of our competitors and we must find a strategy that will place us well above these competitors if we want to outpace them in the marketplace."

A stealth team was formed that developed a very different strategy, which has a much higher probability of achieving supremacy. The strategy that they developed is based on the following observations that they foresaw about the Future Business Arena.

- Since people will be under more and more time pressure, they will have less time to shop. Therefore, a supremacy strategy should give customers the possibility to shop by whatever method is convenient to them. This would include shopping in person, by phone, fax, or over the Internet.

- Although most people are willing to buy packaged goods sight unseen, they usually want to "see and feel" fresh goods such as meat, fish, fruit, and vegetables.

- Some people are quite willing to come to the store to get their food, but more and more people have less and less time to do so.

- Going through cashiers is also time consuming and unproductive. A quicker method of paying for groceries would be welcomed.

- Shopping twice a week, too, is a pain and reducing this frequency would be an added benefit.

With these observations in hand, the team then created a new game that a potential "stealth" entrant would use to attain supremacy in the food retailing sandbox. The new game has a dramatically different set of rules:

- Stores will no longer be fifty to seventy-five thousand square feet but rather in the range of twenty-five to thirty thousand square feet.

- Stores will no longer be rectangular in shape, but circular.

- Traffic will be in one direction, moving around a circle instead of moving up and down aisles, often in opposite directions.

- Non-perishable items will be displayed – with only one sample on display – on shelves arranged inside the circle.

- Fresh goods will be displayed in separate "cavities" built on the perimeter of the outside wall.

- These areas will be staffed by an "expert" in each domain, such as a butcher at the meat counter, similarly at the fish, produce, and fruit counters.

- In fact, the entire store's décor will have a "theme" to give it a distinctive "look and feel" to make shopping an "experience" rather than a task.

- There will be a number of smaller "satellite" stores located strategically around each neighborhood, replenished by the hub store on a daily basis.

- Customers will be able to shop in a number of ways:

  + At the "hub" store

  + By phone, fax, or the Internet

  + Pick-up can be at the hub stores or one of the satellite stores

  + The non-perishable products could be delivered automatically once a month, and one goes to the store for the fresh goods when needed

- A plastic card will also track your purchases and warn you when you might need refills.

How will all this be paid for? A self-service scanner attached to every shelf reads the bar code on the product and keeps a running count of your purchases, thus eliminating the need to wait in line at the cash counter.

Our CEO client was so impressed by this strategy that he decided to embrace it and immediately authorized a pilot store to be built to test the concept. If it proves successful, the strategy will be deployed in all corners of their sandbox over the next few years. Be on the lookout for this new store in your neighborhood soon.

One-Step Real Estate Transactions

If you've ever bought real estate, you are aware of the multitude of tasks necessary to complete the transaction. Another of our clients is in the midst of changing that game in a dramatic manner. That client has been, until now, a title insurance company. Every real estate transaction requires that the "title" of the property – in other words, ownership – be free and clear of liens, thus the moniker "title insurance company." Today, the game is played this way:

- The real estate agent contacts the title insurance company and asks for a "search" of the "title."

- The title insurance company goes to municipal archives and does a manual search of past transactions to ascertain that there are no encumbrances on the property in question.

- The real estate agent then has to coordinate a number of other activities before the sale can be consummated.

  These include:

  - Arranging for an inspection of the property to insure that it is in good shape and that there are no structural flaws

  - Arranging for the financing of the property through a bank or mortgage lender

  - Arranging for a lawyer or notary to prepare all the documents that need to be signed

. . . plus a dozen or more such tasks. Our client is about to change that game radically. Using our process, this company formulated a new strategy that could make it, over time, the focal point of every real estate transaction in the country. The ultimate goal of this new strategy is to be the *"transaction manager"* of all real estate transfers that happen in the United States. In the very near future, real estate agents will be able to go to one source – our client – to obtain all these services. Furthermore, when a seller decides to put a property up for sale, he or she will be able to have many of these services performed in *advance*, thus accelerating the consummation of the transaction. An example would be the inspection the "transaction manager" would have done before any buyer is found. Our client would then give that buyer a seal of approval that the property is in acceptable condition. A visual illustration of this new strategy is shown below.

Closing Room & Transaction Manager

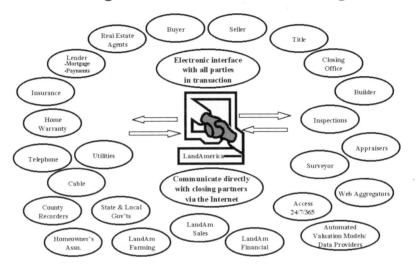

Images "Anywhere, Anytime"

Since Sony announced in 1984 the development of a "digital" camera, the photographic world has not been the same. That announcement sent tremors throughout the industry and was a wake-up call for companies like Kodak and Polaroid. In fact, Kodak is still feeling the aftershocks and so it was for our client as well, since they are manufacturers of equipment that converts "negatives" into "hard copy" photo images. "Digital" images displayed on screens, instead of hard copy, are a death threat to such a company. This client, therefore, had been scrambling for several years to find another strategy. Wisely, it had made a few acquisitions of a number of small companies that were dabbling in this new digital world. Unfortunately, all these entities were operating in their own *separate* worlds with little, if any, contact with each other. All that changed when they assembled to go through our process.

During that process, members of the group came to similar conclusions as to what the Future Business Arena would be. The main conclusion was that, in the future, people will probably want to see their images in both digital and analog (hard copy) formats. In other words, there will still be life for analog imaging equipment. The next realization was that they were the only company that had expertise in *both* sandboxes. Furthermore, they concluded that the game in the future will be played very differently than it is today and that their future competition will not come from their current competitors but rather from a group of "stealth" companies that were not on their radar screens.

Their view of the Future Business Arena is that images will be captured with either analog or digital devices, transmitted somewhere else, and displayed in either analog or digital formats, or both. At the capture and display extremities, the competitors would no longer be Kodak or Fuji but instead Sony, Hewlett-Packard, Epson, Canon, Sharp, and several others. The transmission stage, which will occur over the Internet or telephone lines and even through cable, would attract yet another class of competitors. These would consist of the telecoms of the world and others, such as AOL Time-Warner, and cable TV operators. All this to say, it will be a dramatically different sandbox.

Our client's new strategy? Achieve supremacy in this sandbox by developing equipment that can ease the capture and display of images in either analog *or* digital formats. An example is a new product that they conceived from their use of the "stealth" concept.

Imagine yourself at Walt Disney World® taking pictures of your children at the various rides and attractions. Now you would like Grandma to see how much fun your kids are having. Using a "cameraphone" developed by this company, you simply press a button and your pictures are immediately transmitted over a wireless network to Grandma's PC or television. Grandma experiences your children's delight remotely, but instantly. Or for high quality *prints* your family can enjoy now and later, drop your files at a one-hour photo booth and your pictures are printed out in a standard "analog" format.

Images. Anywhere. Anytime.

Several Homes, Same Developer

Another of our clients is one of the largest developers of homes in the United States. To date, the residential property game is played in the following manner:

- Developers "specialize" in certain categories of home building, such as stand-alone housing, apartments, condos, custom built, assisted living, and so forth.

- Most developers build what they call "communities," which include parks, recreation centers, shopping centers, medical facilities, bike paths, walking trails, and so forth.

- They also specialize by price category, such as low-end, mid-range, and high-end homes.

- They are always searching out new parcels of land for future projects.

- They control the design of these homes but contract the actual building to outside firms.

- Many operate in several geographic markets.

- They build model homes as tantalizers to lure prospective buyers.

- The industry is highly fragmented and no single competitor has more than 2 percent of the total market.

This game is about to be changed dramatically. Our client, also using the stealth concept, determined that supremacy and a significantly much larger market share could be obtained by developing a strategy that would capitalize on an aspect of the business that is not considered today. This is the realization that at various stages of their lives, people want different types of homes. Therefore, a developer that could offer a spectrum of homes built to the changing needs of consumers would have a good chance of keeping these buyers during their entire life span, thus attaining supremacy in the home building sandbox. This company believes that by building a national, or even international, brand associated with an excellent customer experience, it can develop customer loyalty for a lifetime.

Generally, the following represents the evolution of a couple's housing needs over their lifetime:

- Upon marriage, they usually want a "starter" home or an apartment, located close to where they work.

- With the arrival of children, they now want a larger home with access to community services like shopping centers, medical clinics, and recreation parks.

- If their careers take off, they may wish to move into a larger home in a more affluent part of town.

- They may even be transferred to another city but would like to reside in a home similar to the one they currently live in.

- When the children grow up and leave for college, they want to "downsize" into a home that requires less effort to maintain.

- Upon retirement, they may move to Florida or some other location and live in a condo in a retirement or gated community.

This is the strategy that our client is in the process of deploying. The company will start building communities of homes to satisfy the evolving lifestyle needs of their customers. Their intent is to be the only developer that their customers buy homes from throughout their lives. Today, as customers move from one lifestyle to another, they also move from one developer to another, sometimes with unsatisfactory results. Our client concluded that if customers are satisfied with the first "starter" home that they purchase, there is a high probability that these customers will prefer buying their second, third, and even fourth homes from the same developer instead of taking a risk on a new, unknown vendor.

The strategy: Once a customer, forever a customer.

Observations

After more than two dozen experiences with the "stealth" competitor approach to the formulation of a future strategy for an enterprise, here are some observations we have made:

- Every client to date has concluded that the Future Business Arena will be dramatically different from the current sandbox.

- Every client has concluded that the lines of demarcation between sandboxes are getting more and more blurred.

- Every client has identified new potential "stealth" competitors that could enter their sandbox and make life extremely difficult for them.

- Every client has concluded that the "stealth" scenarios developed during our process were realistic and that some organization would pursue such a strategy if they chose not to do so themselves.

- Every client ended up altering their current strategy dramatically to incorporate many, if not all, of the elements of the "stealth" strategy.

How does one go about deciding whether or not it makes sense to adopt part or all of a stealth strategy? The answer to this question, in our view, is the mastery of the concepts of *Strategic Thinking. Strategic Thinking* is the only competitive advantage a CEO and the executive team have over their competitors. To out-think their competitors, not to out-muscle them, in the marketplace is what leads to competitive supremacy.

CEO Interview

Charles Foster
Chairman & Chief Executive Officer

Ted Chandler
Chief Operating Officer

LandAmerica Financial Group, Inc.

> **"We are much more going to go in our own direction,
> full of 'competitors be damned,'
> than we were prior to the DPI process."**
>
> *– Ted Chandler*

Title insurance. To most of us it's just one of those details that come up in the blur of closing a real estate transaction. But to LandAmerica, it's their bread and butter. Or was – until a startling revelation occurred as the company's managers went through DPI's *Strategic Thinking* and *e-Strategy Processes*.

Currently, LandAmerica Financial Group, Inc., is the second largest U.S. supplier of title insurance policies at about $2 billion in revenues. The company is the product of the merging of two large competitors, Lawyer's Title and the

Commonwealth family of companies, in February of 1998.

As mergers go, this one went quite well, as CEO Charlie Foster describes: "There were some good cultural fits and we brought them together. We went through a year of a robust economy, which helped, but then the world had been changing and continued to change. I believe our entire management team was looking for more cohesion than we had been able to articulate. We had completed a lot of projects with regard to the merger and systems, and organizational structures need-ed to be changed but we weren't sending a consistent internal message regarding growth strategies in the face of emerging technologies. We were just saying, here we're two companies that used to do something. How do we do it together? We got by that and there was this company-wide hunger, this need, this management imperative, to be clearer about the future."

In addition, there was a pressing need to deal with some fundamental shifts in the industry. Other mergers. The effects of the Internet. The very nature of how real estate transactions were being done. How would they react? Could they find a way *not* to be reactive, but to be more in charge of their own destiny?

As Foster explains, "It really boiled down to the competitive environment of what was going on in the industry, with how real estate transactions come down. The mortgage originators began to behave differently because of consolidations and capa-bilities afforded them through what I'll call e-commerce or the Internet. There were consolidations going on in our industry and talk of further consolidation. But the state of our business really had to be characterized as one that was more *reactive* than proactive. We were dealing with the world as it was shift-ing, and *responding* to it. Before starting the *Strategic Thinking Process,* I think that would be a fair characterization."

Adds Chief Operating Officer Ted Chandler, "We began to see the limitations of our historical focus on being a single-product vendor of title insurance. We were concerned that this singular focus in a rapidly shifting market positioned us more on the *periphery* of the action than we used to be, and than we wanted to be. We saw the opportunities, but we were not clear on how we should alter our positioning to take advantage of them."

The management team decided to look for objective outside assistance to work out a strategy. But unsatisfactory results from previous encounters with "traditional" content-based consultants led them to look for another solution. DPI's *Strategic Thinking Process* seemed to fit their needs.

"We first concluded that we would like to have a facilitator-enhanced process," Chandler says. "We had experience with consultants that came in and attempted to provide domain expertise, but we knew that the real answers were locked up within us. We were looking for a set of professionals who could help us pull those ideas out. Really, the DPI process, led by a facilitator who transfers the process skills that you need to continue and give momentum to the process, was exactly what we were looking for."

Adds Charlie Foster, "If I could characterize it another way, we were responding to the outside world, including our shareholders and the investment community. And we were, I guess fairly, self-assessing ourselves as having a lack of clarity. We needed a clarity of purpose first of all – what it is we want to do, what our mission really *should* be – and then clarity of thought as to how to approach that goal, that objective of getting *the purpose.* So we were looking for more of a discipline, something that would be continuous, not *the answer* by the *guru du jour.*"

They gathered a LandAmerica management team from a cross-section of locations and disciplines, twenty-five in all, to participate. Right from the start, the *Strategic Thinking* concept clicked.

"The reaction from our people was very positive," Chandler says. "I think there was a desire for this. We, like most companies, had a strategy. We were executing on a strategy but it tended to be more of an implicit strategy that was not being aggressively communicated beyond the executive suite. And the reason is, as Charlie said, there was a bit of a lack of clarity as to how boldly we should be taking advantage of emerging opportunities. When we brought the people together for the work session, I think there was a real buy-in that it was appropriate, and needed."

Despite the fact that the participants had come from many parts of the company and country, the process quickly got them on the same page and moving toward a surprising conclusion. It became immediately apparent that the company might make a major change of direction and Driving Force – creating an opportunity to drastically change the game in their sandbox.

As Chandler explains, "Because this business is largely locally driven and because real estate laws are different, and customs and practices are different, when you pull these people together you find that it takes a while to talk the same language. This is because the business, even though it's under the rubric of title insurance, is actually executed differently depending on your geographic market. So the effort to identify the Driving Force brought on a lot of discussion. And we actually, I think, are unusual among companies that have gone through the DPI process because we have *changed* our Driving Force. After we identified our current Driving Force as Product – title insurance policies – we realized we could really *change the game* if we moved to a *new* Driving Force – User Class."

To put a finer point on it, they would be moving away from being simply a title insurance company, and moving toward providing a wide range of services, all related to the real estate transaction. Instead of selling a single piece of the puzzle, they would eventually manage the entire transaction – a radically different business model.

"The simple truth of the matter," says Charlie Foster, "is that we had been very oriented towards something called a title insurance policy, which, if you peeled it back, had 95 percent *information* value versus 5 percent *insurance* value. But our current thesis is to try to respond to what the customer *really* wants. And the customer, no matter if it's a lender, a realtor, a builder-developer, or an attorney – our basic customer sets – what we think they want is a facilitated transaction, not just the title insurance. And so we're putting ourselves in a position to be that concierge, to be the facilitator, to provide that *seamless transaction.* And we're starting to call ourselves a *transaction manager,* as a simple phrase, as opposed to a title insurance fulfiller."

"The primary piece of it is that we had to get away from thinking of ourselves as just a title insurance company," Chandler says. "So our sandbox is that *we proactively provide services in the information, assurance, fiduciary, and settlement segments of the real estate business. And we intend to be the preeminent provider of seamless transactions and value-added knowledge through economical, time sensitive, and customized solutions.* That combined statement of our future strategic profile does a number of things. It focuses people on the fact that when we talk about *information, assurance, fiduciary, and settlement,* then *title insurance* tucks into *assurance.* It's just one of a series of guarantee products that we can provide. And when we speak to a sandbox that encompasses providing the information needs of the real estate industry, we're talking about, in fact, a *very* large market opportunity. That articulation of the sandbox and aggressive development of multiple products in that area, coupled with our intent *to be the preeminent provider of seamless transactions,* leads us into an e-strategy emphasis and the need to build a different profile than we had been pursuing."

A change of Driving Force mandates a corresponding change in the Areas of Excellence to be developed and nurtured. LandAmerica's people do not perceive this to be a major problem, as these areas are not entirely new to the company's culture. It simply means a change of emphasis.

As Chandler sees it, "Our main Area of Excellence is Market Knowledge, which is really an aggregation of local market knowledge. To support that we will also need to concentrate more on information management and technology. Even though we're in the 'insurance business,' that is very much misleading. We're an information management company and that is really our business. And then thirdly is Internet technology, and that is a skill set, not just purchased goods. It is an area of focus, and it is highlighted under our future strategic profile management because we need to leverage it to a significantly greater degree."

To get their arms around the role that the Internet might play in the future, they decided to use DPI's *e-Strategy Process*, again with very surprising results.

Says Foster, "We didn't realize, going in, the kinds of things we'd come up with and how central they would be to our new strategy. I looked at it as a scenario of 'Gee, I don't know enough; this is education. Let's do it!' You know, you have these natural anxieties and fears that somebody knows something you don't know. So that's why we went into that process. The almost immediate outcome of that is that now we don't even call this e-strategy. *This is just strategy.* It was its own separate project at the outset. In fact, now it's one of our major Critical Issues to the overall development of strategy. So we're attempting to learn and build and develop strategy based upon what I call the evolution of Internet-based commerce.

"We had, in our previous fragmented approach to the Internet, responded to one of our customer sets by building a part of our company – which we called LandAmerica One-Stop – to try to respond to what the customer was saying. But we were doing it looking through the eyeglasses of a title insurer. So we hadn't thought of everything. In fact, we weren't, from a technology standpoint, very far along in terms of connectivity. We had struggled with that. Because of the DPI process, we immediately recognized the need to look at it in the broader context."

That broader context, of course, was the new, more expansive strategy the company had embarked on. Given that their products are essentially information products and that the thousands of potential customers are located literally everywhere, e-commerce would play a central role as the concept developed.

The *e-Strategy Process* allowed them to create a realistic and comprehensive design for an e-commerce solution that would precisely fit their new business model – complete with definitions of specific applications and their requirements. What really made the whole e-commerce concept gel, though, was the transformation they saw take place through the "Killer.com" segment of the process.

"Part of what we had done during the process was to engage ourselves in two or three exercises. But one of them was much more than an exercise – it was something about building a whole new model. And through the Killer.com we came up with an approach that turned the light on and we said, 'You know, this sounds exotic but it really is what we're trying to do.' It's just a way of explaining it, of giving it a complete definition," Foster states.

The result is the game-changing "Transaction Manager" concept, brought to market, in part, by the Internet portal described in greater detail in Chapter 9. This breakthrough model will take years to bring to fruition, but LandAmerica wasted no time getting started. Within weeks, they made a strategic acquisition that would supply a critical piece of the new business.

Chandler explains: "We – almost immediately out of the box, after having our phase two session, once our future strategic profile was set, once the Strategic Filter was delivered – applied that filter to several pressing opportunities. We zeroed in on this one particular target company, called Primis. We very boldly acquired the company, and we have incorporated that business into one of our most important market segments. So there was this absolute direct, not indirect, linkage between the development of that Strategic Filter and us pulling the trigger on a major initiative.

"Primis embodies our movement into this transaction management space in a key market segment. What we got with that company was a whole array of valuation products we were not offering and market knowledge of where innovation was needed. We also were able to get technology that was specific to those products. But what we had, and what we saw, and what has proved out, is that the acquired technology was readily adaptable to be our primary e-commerce front-end with respect to this one very large market segment. So when we bought Primis, we merged it into one of our companies that was operating in the same market but didn't have the same set of tools. And combined, we are very, very well positioned to be the transaction manager for our largest, most demanding customers.

"I can actually say, unequivocally, that we would not have bought Primis but for the DPI process. I mean that just flat out, because prior to DPI, we were not looking to expand into, essentially, another line of business – the valuation products line of business. And even if we had been, we would not have done it at this level of financial commitment."

Because of the complexity of the new LandAmerica business model, it will take some time to develop it and mold it into a complete, integrated operation. Primis is an important piece of the puzzle. Yet despite the challenges inherent in creating a new game, Foster and his team are confident that the concept is sound and that the market is moving toward using this type of service. The journey has also completely changed their perception of the game, the rules, and the nature of competition in their space.

"We haven't completed them yet," says Chandler, "but the transaction management tactics that we're bringing to the table will have the effect of changing the game. We're doing business in a way that's different than any of our natural competitors. We are actually counter-intuitively positioning ourselves so that we will even sell our competitors' products. We are moving into the transaction intersection to manage the transaction, and, if our customer wants to use our competitor for the title order, then we're going to do that. So what changes the rules of play is that all of a sudden when a customer chooses us, they're not making a choice on one major title company versus another major title company where the differences across the country may not always be apparent or real. They're making a choice that they want a manager of that transaction who will then use the fulfillment entities that are best in class – best in class being defined by the customer or in the absence of being defined by the customer, defined as quicker, better, cheaper. This will fundamentally change the game and the rules of play because we do not see our other traditional competitors positioning themselves in a way that they would forego the title insurance order.

"As a result, we are less obsessed with our traditional competitors than we were before. I think one of the benefits of going through the DPI process is that you become more confident in the direction of the company, and therefore you're less reactive to their 'me-too' type strategies. And the other piece of this is that we recognize that our traditional competitors, in this brave new world, are perhaps not our *real* competitors. That comes out of the Killer.com evaluation. So we are much more going to go in *our own direction*, full of 'competitors be damned,' than we were prior to the DPI process."

Throughout the next couple of years, a new type of company will emerge, although pieces of the model may change as ideas are tested and adjusted to fit the evolving marketplace. Says CEO Foster, "We have come up with what we think is a pretty good game plan. Now, it isn't proven out and it changes from time to time. In fact, one of the beauties of this whole DPI effort is the fact that it is a continuum. *Strategic Thinking* is just that, a continuum of thinking."

Where would they be had they continued on their former course? Foster puts it succinctly: "We probably would have been much more on the target end of the range than the shooting end."

10

The Strategic Thinking Process: From Strategy Creation to Deployment

**"Winning companies will be
those that out-think,
not out-muscle,
their competitors."**

The Logistics Of The Strategic Thinking Process

The first and foremost responsibility of any CEO is to formulate a strategy for the organization in order to give its employees a sense of direction and harness their energy towards the goal of *supremacy* over its competitors. The process that assists a CEO in this endeavor is one that is proprietary to DPI, which we call *Strategic Thinking*. Here is an overview of how the process proceeds.

Phase 1

This first phase is a half-day introductory session with two activities. First, we give the group an overview of the concepts and process so that they are comfortable with these. The second activity is to introduce our Strategic Input Survey, in which the participants are asked to respond to a set of questions prior to the main three-day session that follows a month later. Their answers become the "raw material" for the next session. These responses are sent to us for editing and collating. Our goal is to encourage thoughtful attention to these key questions and extract meaningful answers as opposed to simply "brainstorming" answers on the spur of the moment.

Phase 2

Strategic Thinking Process

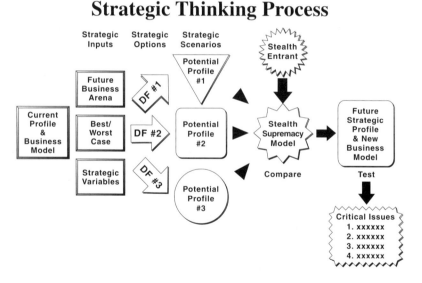

This session starts with the construction of a "snapshot" of the company in its present form. This consists of identifying the characteristics that are common to all the company's products, all the company's customers, all the company's market segments, and all the company's geographic markets. By identifying the characteristics that are *common* across these four elements of a company's profile, we can then uncover the company's *current* Driving Force, its *current* Business Concept, and its *current* Areas of Excellence. Gaining agreement about the company's *current* profile is the starting point of *strategy formulation.*

The next step in this process is to conduct a scan of the external environment and determine what the Future Business Arena, that we will find ourselves in, will look like. Once we are reasonably comfortable with that "picture" of the future, we can more specifically identify the *strategic variables* that will play for or against us in that arena. This will help us circumscribe the "sandbox" over which we want to establish supremacy.

Now for the fun part: the creation of a "stealth competitor," a concept that we described in Chapter 1. Which stealth competitor could step into that sandbox and attempt to establish supremacy for itself and create havoc for us? One team is given this assignment and they develop a specific strategy and business model that such a "stealth" entrant would deploy against us with the intent of gaining supremacy.

The next step is then for us to identify which components of our business could be the Driving Force of our future strategy. Companies can usually identify two or three areas that could be the engine of their future strategy. We then take each of these "possible" Driving Forces and develop "profiles" of what we would emphasize more or emphasize less under each one. The development of these scenarios then allows the CEO and the management team to choose the Driving Force that will best all current competitors, as well as any new "stealth" entrant into our sandbox.

The final step in this first work session is then to surface the Critical Issues that the management team will need to address and resolve over time in order to attain, maintain, or enhance our supremacy in our chosen sandbox.

Phase 3

This one-day work session is dedicated to the construction of *strategic objectives.* These are different from that of operational objectives by function, which most companies already do quite well, but are usually extrapolations of past performance – numbers – into the future.

Strategic objectives are different. They do not pertain to functions within a company but rather to a company's future profile, which consists of products, customers, industry segments, and geographic markets. Strategic objectives are the "hills" that we must defend or capture in these four areas that will make our strategy succeed or fail.

Critical Issues: The Bridge To Strategy Deployment

At this point, our clients get to work on the "Critical Issues." These are the handful of essential initiatives that form the basis of the new strategy. These Critical Issues are one of the most crucial outputs from the *Strategic Thinking Process.* They are the keys to successful deployment because they have been chosen and agreed upon by those who will carry out the strategy. Once decided, these issues are assigned to individuals to drive them to conclusion. This is where the rubber hits the road – and where the commitment you have developed among these managers will flesh out the strategy and make it happen.

Identification Of Critical Issues

Critical Issues are the bridge between the current profile and the future strategic profile of an organization that management has deliberately decided to pursue. The direction of the organization has been decided and managing that direction begins. Managing that direction on an ongoing basis means management of the Critical Issues that stem from four key areas:

- Structure

- Systems/Processes

- Skills/Competencies

- Compensation

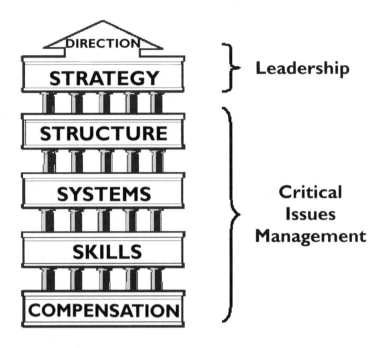

Critical Issues That Relate To Structure

One of our clients recently asked us a very good question: Since most corporations are organized in a similar manner, does that mean that they have a similar strategy?

After all, most companies have a marketing function, a sales function, a production function, an engineering function, an accounting function, an IT function, a human resource function, and so on. Most are also organized in a similar manner geographically with a domestic operational unit and an international unit separated by country, or groups of countries, into regions. They may further be organized by product, by country which leads to some form of "matrix" organization. Therefore, *similar organization, similar strategy.*

Nothing could be further from the truth! Although organizational structures look as if they stem from the same business model, there are some important nuances that make the various functions behave in very different modes. A correlating example is people. Although all men wear suits and all women wear dresses, no two women or two men behave in the same way.

The same is true in business. Although all companies "wear" the same clothes – organization – no two organizations behave in the same manner in the marketplace. In fact, if you were to look more carefully, you would detect that, although companies use the same words or titles, they are in fact organized in a very *different* manner.

The underlying element that determines an organization's structure is the concept of Driving Force, which is at the root of every business strategy.

Take, for example, 3M, Johnson & Johnson, and Caterpillar, the examples used earlier. 3M is organized around "applications" it uncovers for its knowledge of polymer chemistry – its *Driving Force.* As a result, it has a Post-it® division, a Masking Tape division, a Video Tape division, a Film division . . . which are all different applications of its root polymer chemistry. Each division has its own sales, marketing, and manufacturing functions since these tend to require *different skills* from one application to another, using *different* methods to get to market. Some divisions sell direct, some use agents and distributors. Some make end-use products, some make components for other companies' products.

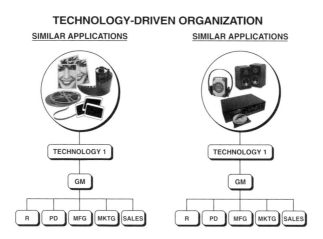

TECHNOLOGY-DRIVEN ORGANIZATION

Caterpillar, on the other hand, uses the same titles and words but is organized in a very different manner. Since it pursues a *Product-driven* strategy – earthmoving machines – the company is organized around different product categories. They have a Large Machine Division, a Mid-size Machine Division, a Small Machine Division, and recently added a Compact Machine Division. The manufacturing is decentralized, whereby different functions are centralized and broken down geographically with a General Manager for each geographic market. This is done to accommodate Caterpillar's unique network of Independent Dealers, which is their chosen way to market.

Johnson & Johnson is not organized like either of these other two. Its strategy is "satisfying the health needs of doctors, nurses, patients, and mothers" – *a User Class driven* strategy. As such, it is organized around where these four individuals are accessed. As a result, it has two divisions – a Hospital Division since this is where doctors, nurses, and patients are found, and it has a Consumer Division, which is where the mother is found. Manufacturing is thus centralized while each division has its own sales and marketing organizations. All the products aimed at doctors, nurses, and patients go through the Hospital division and all the products aimed at mothers go through the Consumer division.

There was a fad in the 1970s and 1980s to reorganize and restructure companies. After the reorganization, the most difficult question to answer became: "Now that we are reorganized, where are we going?"

In our view, structure follows strategy. The organization structure of the business must support the direction of that business. We have further learned that each Driving Force requires a slightly different organization structure.

Critical Issues That Relate To Processes/Systems

The next discussion that leads to Critical Issues is one that revolves around the subject of "systems." Many companies today have purchased sophisticated and costly electronic information systems only to find out some time later that the systems are not supportive of the company's business strategy. Again, our view is that all information systems must be aligned with the direction of the organization and that there are usually issues that surface in the area of systems or processes.

Critical Issues That Relate To Skills/Competencies

When an organization changes its direction, this change will usually require the acquisition of a new set of skills. These can be developed, but frequently they do not reside in-house and must be acquired, thus giving rise to another set of Critical Issues. For example, when LandAmerica adopted a new strategy that required more Internet capabilities, one of the most pressing Critical Issues was the acquisition of a company that had the necessary capabilities in that area.

Critical Issues That Relate To Compensation

In spite of all the titles or power you might think you have over people, my experience has convinced me that people do not do what you *want* them to do; people do what they are *paid* to do. If your strategy says that you want your people to behave in a certain manner, but your compensation system rewards them to do something different, I can virtually assure you that at the end of the year they will have done what they were *paid* to do and not what you *wanted* them to do.

As a result, another area of discussion that raises Critical Issues is the subject of compensation, to ensure that the compensation of key individuals is geared to supporting the strategy and direction of the business.

Around these four specific areas – structure, systems, skills, and compensation – a number of Critical Issues are identified and assigned to specific individuals for resolution. The expected results are articulated, the macro action steps are listed, other people that need to be involved are assigned to each team, and completion and review dates are established. These Critical Issues then become "the plan" for the organization, and it is the ongoing management and resolution of these issues that makes the CEO's vision a reality over time. It is how the strategy is deployed successfully.

Closing The Loop

At this point, you might be wondering how all the concepts presented tie together into a cohesive whole.

The rectangle at the top of the graphic above represents the output of our *Strategic Thinking Process.* The strategic profile is a description of what an organization wants to look like at some point in the future. The inside of the rectangle contains the content of this picture. The Critical Issues are the bridge that needs to be crossed in order to go from what the company looks like today to what it wants to look like tomorrow. Next comes planning time.

The Operational Plan

The next task is to examine the organization's current activities and decide which products, customers, and markets need to be improved or modified. Moreover, one must identify those that need to be eliminated because they no longer fit the vision of what the company is trying to become.

One of the most difficult decisions we find management having to make, if they do not have what we call a "strategic filter," is not what to do but rather what *not to do anymore.* This is because there is always someone telling management to "hang in" a little longer – that the corner is about to come but, in fact, it never does. During the operational planning stage, these decisions become easier to make because all participants have agreed on that strategic filter and that those activities no longer fit their aspiration of the type of company they are trying to build.

Said Jack Messman, former CEO of Union Pacific Resources and now CEO of Novell:

> "By agreeing to a strategy, you also agree to what you're *not* going to do. This avoids wasting time and resources on activities that do not support the strategy. After using the DPI Process, our people became more focused on success and stopped debating alternatives."

The Strategic Plan

In our view, a strategic plan is one that will alter the "look" of an organization in the future. The key elements that will alter the "look" of a company in the future are the new products, new customers, and new markets that the company wants to add to that look. A plan now needs to be constructed to make these happen.

Our experience shows that if you want to give birth to brand new activities (products, markets, and acquisitions), it is wise to have people other than those who are running your current businesses "midwife" these projects to birth. The rationale is simple: Those running your current businesses have a locomotive on their hands, and keeping that engine on track will require all their time and energy. As such, it is wise to have new activities managed outside the normal structure of the current business.

The Strategic Profile Is The Target
For All Decisions

As illustrated, the strategic profile becomes the target for all the decisions that are made in the organization. Plans and decisions that fit inside the frame of this profile are pursued, and those that do not fit, are not.

Phase 4: Critical Issues Meeting

One CEO client recently said to this author:

"You DPI guys are no more than *strategic enforcers.* Because we scheduled a meeting with you, we show up. Otherwise, we'd find something else to do. And when we show up, we know what questions you are going to ask. So we work our butts off because no one wants to go to that meeting and report 'no progress.'" I thought this was a very good way of describing our involvement in the *deployment* of the strategy as well as in its *formulation.*

Phase 4 consists of two quarterly, half-day meetings with the CEO and the management team to review progress on the Critical Issues. At these meetings, the "owner" of each issue is expected to give a report of progress. These meetings give the CEO an opportunity to:

- assess the progress, or non-progress, on each issue.

- determine whether the issue is "on-track" or "off-track."

- judge whether the work on each issue is proceeding at the proper pace.

- remove any obstacles that the owners and their teams are running into.

- make any midcourse corrections.

Phase 5: Review/Revisit Session

Some ten to twelve months after Phase 2, most clients want to have a review, or revisit, of their previous conclusions.

Because these conclusions were based on a certain number of assumptions as to what might or might not occur in the environment, most CEOs want to revisit these assumptions to see which proved to be right and which ones wrong. This reassessment allows the client to fine-tune the strategy and occasionally pick up a Critical Issue or two that were missed the first time through the process.

Conclusion

"Thinking," said Henry Ford, "is a difficult activity. That is why so many people don't practice that habit."

CEO Interview

Harald Stolzenberg
President
Juvena/LaPrairie

"What we wanted was not a Juvena strategy, or a LaPrairie strategy. We wanted a *corporate* strategy."

– *Harald Stolzenberg*

"In our industry, the brand is almost like a cult. You have to *live* the cult," explains Harald Stolzenberg, President of Swiss cosmetics firm Juvena/LaPrairie. The company, owned by Beiersdorf Group, is a world leader in a market – anti-aging facial cosmetics – that is certain to grow through the coming decades. Its product lines, Juvena and LaPrairie, are well known among upscale women everywhere. As in most consumer products companies, the day-to-day focus is on building those brands with nearly religious fervor. In high-end cosmetics, this is especially true.

Though the company was healthy, profitable, and expanding in the late '90s, management had begun to feel that its growth was becoming somewhat unfocused, with too many opportunities and projects vying for limited resources. And although its *brand* strategies were clear, the time came to bring the two brand groups and upper management together to create a well-defined *corporate* strategy.

"One group had Juvena, and another group, LaPrairie, in mind, which is what they are supposed to be doing," Stolzenberg says. "We also had people thinking about other projects. What we wanted was not a *Juvena* strategy or a *LaPrairie* strategy. We wanted a *corporate* strategy. We wanted something that says, apart from the needs of individual brands or projects, this is what the *whole company* needs. That was very important. We needed to get people away from the daily business of promoting their own brands, and for a few days step back and ask what is best for the *company* in the future. The hope was that in the end, maybe even somebody from Juvena would say, for example, 'I think we should invest more into LaPrairie at this point in time.' We were getting to the point where we said we have to very clearly define what we do. Do we want to develop the fragrance business? Do we want to promote certain countries more than others? What kinds of people do we need to add? We had such a number of projects and issues that were arising more out of growth than out of some problem. Everybody was feeling we were doing too many things. Clearly, we needed a strategy to help us decide which of our *real* opportunities we should concentrate on."

The immediate question was how to go about creating this strategy. One approach would have been to hire a traditional management consultant to come in and develop a strategic plan. But the company's people were "consulted out," in Stolzenberg's view.

"When we re-engineered the business and changed the whole company over to SAP, we had consultants all over the place. They take up a lot of time; you always see the same charts. So when we decided to develop this strategy we had two choices – hire McKinsey or whatever, or find someone with a methodology to enable us to do it ourselves. The whole management team agreed that if you want to have a corporate strategy, you should be disciplined enough to do it yourself. Yet we are a very creative team, which has great advantages, but it leads to *too many* ideas. So we brought in Marnix Coopman, a DPI Partner in Switzerland, to facilitate the *Strategic Thinking Process.* That gave us the method and discipline to stay on track."

The company put together a team from across the business and set about preparing the basic information required in the DPI process. Stolzenberg began to see a coming together of the brand groups even during the prep work before the core process sessions.

As Stolzenberg recalls, "There was a lot of cross-work, especially in the preparation time before the first meeting and the second. The crucial time was before the first meeting. There was, understandably, a kind of critical attitude among some of the people: 'Why are we doing this? Is this going to be just another consultant telling us what to do?' But after the first day when the method was explained, there was a lot of positive discussion among the people. Then I think everyone came to the meeting extremely well prepared."

The DPI process essentially enabled the company's management to examine its resources and capabilities in detail through this thorough and disciplined analysis, and come to a unified understanding of what makes Juvena/LaPrairie a unique, distinctive enterprise. Based on those conclusions, a comprehensive strategy was developed. One of the pivotal points was the choice of what DPI calls the Driving Force, as explained earlier, one of ten that are set out in the process. The Driving Force is the single most important element in the company that propels it to the well-defined set of products, customers, and markets it will pursue.

Says Stolzenberg, "Before thinking it through, we all, including myself, thought we were a *Product*-driven company. After all, we spend every day thinking about our *products*. This was probably the most difficult part, but Marnix Coopman took the time to help us think it out."

As a small company in a very fragmented business, the central question became: What Driving Force has enabled, or will enable the company to compete and grow against competitors as large as L'Oreal and many others? Through the DPI process, the group came to the unanimous conclusion that they are not *Product*-driven at all, but rather *Know-how*-driven. Its unique edge in the marketplace is its exceptional know-how in creating high-end skincare products, primarily in the anti-aging niche. It is this particular know-how, the team reasoned, that has resulted in its most successful products, created a loyal consumer following, and set Juvena/LaPrairie apart from other cosmetics companies. This know-how stems from an in-depth understanding of skin cells, the stresses they undergo in aging, and effective treatments to counteract these damaging elements. This difference would at once define what kinds of products, markets, and customers it would – and would *not* – pursue in the future.

Of Juvena/LaPrairie's unique know-how, Stolzenberg says, "It's mainly in R&D, where the D is bigger than the R. It is basically product development, including marketing know-how. So we had to define that and say, for instance, 'Our parent is one of the leading companies in the world for basic scientific research in this area. How can we leverage that and cooperate better?' As a result, we decided to hire people, who we called hunters, who now work with our parent company to discover what new know-how we can gather in this specific area and turn into products. Instead of just saying we want to develop whatever products our competitors do, we decided to really expand our know-how to create *unique* new products.

"A lot of this know-how comes from discovering the thousands of ingredients that are already there but where the potential has not been recognized, or by finding new combinations that help deal with skin problems. That is because the ingredients are quite regulated and new ones do not come along very often. That is where we want to become an excellent or even *unique* know-how company.

"The other thing we said was we have so much know-how

in our company, maybe we can use it in cooperation with other partners. Maybe we can have strategic partnerships where we are more than a third party manufacturer, which we always did because we have quite an effective factory. That has now resulted in two major companies cooperating with us where we develop, consult, produce, and sometimes even take on the logistic part. That has had an enormous effect. For instance, the R&D costs, which are very high for a smaller company, are distributed better and we can afford more highly qualified people, which, again, will help our own brands.

"We have expanded our R&D as a *clear result* of analyzing our organization through the DPI process and realizing what would be critical to our future. We have rebuilt the laboratories and hired four or five additional people in the meantime. We are building up the R&D know-how as part of our long-term strategy. We really said that even if we have to over-invest, this is essential to our long-term survival.

"That is the core of the strategy. And that's where we have really invested. Now we are much ahead of where we were a year ago. Probably the *next* most important part is that *everybody accepted* that and stopped criticizing when we invest money there. Everybody realized that this is necessary to our survival in this environment. Everybody is behind the investment in R&D. Absolutely."

Another important step in the process is the forging of a concise Business Concept. Everyone has seen mission statements, all of which seek to communicate what the company's all about. Most fall short of a useful definition. But the DPI process requires the construction of a Business Concept that defines a future direction in detail and creates Strategic Filters for decision making company-wide.

"We could have easily written down a five-page Business Concept," says Stolzenberg, "but Marnix Coopman drove us to get it down to a few sentences. When we really condensed it we saw why this part is so important. This is the precise expression of our strategy. It guides us in knowing what we have to do about it."

The Business Concept is as follows:

> We will leverage our unique know-how by searching or combining technologies to produce and market innovative face-care products with emphasis on anti-aging. We will do this by cascading to other care-related categories, faster and better than the competition. We will cater only to demanding women with beauty and well-being needs that buy in selective distribution worldwide. We want competent and motivated people around the world to reach our objective and generate the necessary profit, to self-fund our own growth by satisfying our shareholders and our own people. We will prioritize our own brands and consider others, if needed, for critical mass for improving profitability. We must excel in our know-how management by continuously searching for new combinations to launch in a surprisingly new way and earlier than the competition.

The practical value of creating such a statement of purpose is that it serves as a strategic filter for differentiating between essential and non-essential projects and expenditures. Stolzenberg explains, "We now have *strategic filters* and *financial filters.* The strategic filters we arrived at quite fast. For the financial filters we needed a little bit longer. Now all of our projects go through these filters. We are quite tough with ourselves. That means we are sometimes fighting with our own filters, which is good. And I personally think that the *strategic* filter is more important than the *financial* filter, because some of the things we did in the past would have never passed the strategic filter we now have. If you have that kind of self-critique of what you have done, it helps in deciding about new projects. Now when an idea comes up we ask ourselves, 'Should we really do that? Is it in line with our filter?'

"I'll give you an example. We could say, 'Should we develop a new fragrance?' Some of our competitors make fragrances and it's possible for us to do, but it doesn't fit into the filter created by our Business Concept. It doesn't leverage our Know-How Driving Force. In the past we might have just done it, maybe out of enthusiasm or because competitors are doing it. There is always a reason, such as, 'It complements the business,' 'We can use our synergies,' and so on. Now we would probably say, 'That product doesn't fit our strategic filter.' And of course, from time to time we may have to review the filters. They shouldn't be dogma. They shouldn't be the Bible. On the other hand, they should not be changed daily."

Since the completion of the *Strategic Thinking Process*, the company has been diligently working to resolve a set of Critical Issues – the specific steps to implementing the new strategy. The action most central to the strategy was the increased emphasis on product and market development. Much of that effort is well underway. As a next step, Juvena/LaPrairie has decided to use DPI's *Strategic Product Innovation Process* to "keep the hopper full" of new ideas for growth. The company's Business Concept once again will serve as a filter for determining which ideas should be pursued.

"One of the other issues," says Stolzenberg, "was changing our attitude toward classic trade. That was one of the things that we ingested for the first time within the whole group. The marketing people and some others had dealt with it before. But now the whole group knows that this is a threat and an opportunity at the same time. Again, I think what you learn is very often just two sides of the same coin. For example, concentration of trade can run in your favor or can run against you. Last year we had the abolishment of the duty free business in Europe. It was considered a Critical Issue and we have learned how to take advantage as a growth opportunity."

As the company continues to work the Critical Issues, Stolzenberg now feels that Juvena/LaPrairie's people are far more united in their focus than before.

"One of the advantages of this process is that the people who were present and those they have spread the word to are taking a more corporate view of where we should go and invest. They now can look at the company as a whole, not just at their own brand. I can say, very clearly, that this has happened. That alone was worth the effort.

"We are doing well at cooperating and seeing our interdependence," Stolzenberg states. "We all know that if you want to reach a common goal, all the brands have to do well and everybody has to do something for the other. Very obviously, the formulation of the strategy did a great job of that. We can't put it into numbers yet, but there's a general feeling that we all know where we want to go and that has made many things much easier."

CEO Interview

teckwahgroup™

BEST PEOPLE BEST SOLUTIONS

Thomas Chua
Group Deputy Chairman & Managing Director
Teckwah Industrial Corporation Ltd.

> **"The DPI process emphasizes changing the rules and controlling your sandbox. This intrigued us very much and we have done that."**
>
> **– *Thomas Chua***

The story starts this way.

Two guys in a dormitory room write an ingenious software program. People like it and want to buy it. They start a company to market it and develop future enhancements. The company grows. Pretty soon, they're spending a lot of their resources on activities unrelated to software and customer support. Package development. CD production. Order fulfillment. Retail distribution. And on and on. Profits lag and innovation loses momentum as the business gets bogged down in more and more complicated logistics.

Then along comes Teckwah, an entrepreneurial Singapore-based company that provides complete supply chain services, from packaging design through shipping and distribution. The two guys heave a sigh of relief and get back to what they do best – creating software. Their company starts growing again.

Teckwah: From Cardboard Boxes
To Supply Chain Management

The idea of becoming a "complete supply chain management services provider" to the IT industry didn't come to Teckwah out of the blue. The concept developed in stages with the help of DPI's *Strategic Thinking Process.*

Teckwah first opened its doors in 1968 as a printer of cardboard boxes. Under the guidance of founder Chua Seng Tek, father of present Managing Director Thomas Chua, the company did well in Singapore's thriving manufacturing-based economy. After all, most manufactured goods wind up in cardboard boxes. It was a good niche and the company gradually moved on to more sophisticated commercial printing and packaging products as their customers' needs changed.

The company eventually served a variety of markets such as food and beverage, toys, consumer electronics and so on. Fast-forward to 1994, when the company went public.

For a while after the offering, Teckwah continued to prosper. But times were changing and the company was in danger of being left behind. As one packaging printer among many, it found the competitive environment heating up while Singapore was gradually diminishing its emphasis on manufacturing, and moving into the era of the "knowledge-based economy." With a hefty overhead in printing facilities, the company was feeling the pinch.

As Thomas Chua recalls, "In the early '90s we were working very hard to get listed on the Singapore Stock Exchange. We were at the peak of our performance in both top and bottom line at the time of the listing. But we really had not addressed what we would do next. Our planning for the future had all been done based on what we had done in the past – commercial printing and packaging materials. We expanded geographically into China and other regions. But after a while we felt we had lost our direction, and that something had to be done. But what and how? Coincidentally, a letter from Andrew Sng, a DPI Partner in Singapore, hit the right note and we decided to call DPI in. We liked the idea of a process that would guide us to think logically and strategically. I was also looking for a platform where I could involve other levels of staff."

So in 1997, the top three tiers of Teckwah management went through DPI's *Strategic Thinking Process.*

"It was a session that involved all the right people," Chua recalls. "It was because of this team involvement that top management and the next two levels down could understand one another's opinions and thinking better. This enhanced the communication between the top management and the next levels since we were able to use a common language when talking about strategy. The interrelated questions led us to think through the implications of our past, present, and future internal and external environments, and finally arrive at a consolidated picture that captured all of these."

The sessions resulted in a major shift in the focus of Teckwah's business, culminating in the agreement among the management that their Driving Force should change from *Capacity*-driven to *Market*-driven. They would concentrate on one rapidly growing customer segment – the IT industry – and provide those customers with new services that were logical extensions of printing and packaging.

"As we went through the DPI process, we finally realized that in the past we had just banked on our production capacity," Thomas Chua recalls. "But expansion in that kind of business is difficult and expensive because you have to buy more machinery and keep it running at top capacity. So to fill capacity, we would serve anybody we could offer our services to. It became so competitive and all our competitors were doing the same thing. There's no point to trying to keep up the capacity if you don't have the business. So we decided to focus on one or two industries and expand our range of services to them. We studied among the industries we knew and decided that the emerging Information Technology industry, which we were already involved with, had the most potential.So we changed to a *Market* Driving Force. We concentrated on providing higher value services to that niche market and it worked."

At that time, the IT business was in a rapid expansion mode, with an explosion in product development and marketing. Teckwah saw a need for a growing list of services, all related to printing – activities that are not core competencies of their customers. The opportunity was there for the taking – *if* they could effectively make the needed changes in their organization. So, as part of the process, they developed a list of Critical Issues – actions that would be essential to the successful implementation of the new strategy. Foremost among them were attracting top-notch people with knowledge of the industry, and discovering and developing the services that would be most valued by this burgeoning segment.

The business concept that emerged was right on target, the Critical Issues were effectively accomplished over time and the company's range of services – and top and bottom lines – grew. Management today feels that the successful deployment of this strategy was greatly enhanced because of participation in the DPI process by several levels of Teckwah managers.

Says Chua, "Our middle management level understood our strategic profile better because they were involved, and so there was *ownership* in the action plans, and they cascaded the action plans down to their subordinates. Now we have a set of documents, a Strategic Filter, for us to refer to. Whenever we want to invest or make some major decision, we check whether it is in line with our business concept and strategic profile. A good example is that we decided to divest a subsidiary which, although it is profitable, did not fit our strategic profile any more."

As Thomas Chua describes the new strategic direction that emerged from the *Strategic Thinking* sessions, "To a certain extent we changed the rules in our sandbox. As a packaging printer, usually you produce your packaging box in your factory and deliver it to your customer, and they do the final packing. Now, as one example of how we have changed that system, our customers could send their finished products to our factory and we would do the final packaging and fulfillment for them. So this is not a standard practice. We even do the sourcing for the customer in some of the accessory items. So we made a transition from printing to what we now call the supply-chain business."

As the new concept took hold, profitability improved dramatically, as expansion was now far less capital-intensive than growing the printing business had been.

"First of all," Thomas Chua says, "the supply-chain business is more service oriented compared to printing and packaging, which is more production oriented. And when the supply-chain business expands, we don't have to invest heavily in equipment. Investment is more in people and computer systems. So when the business grows, expansion is much less costly."

Staying Agile In A Radically Shifting Environment

Yet, despite all of this success, two unforeseen shifts in Teckwah's external environment – the Asian financial crisis, and a sudden slowdown in IT industry growth –prompted a strategic review in 1999.

Again, Andrew Sng led the Teckwah managers through the DPI process with a very unusual result – a second change of Driving Force! Recognizing that growth in IT and the economy in general had diminished, *and* that Teckwah had developed a sophisticated supply-chain management expertise, they decided to change their Driving Force to *Capability*. The capability, of course, is supply-chain management. The main difference would be the development of an even deeper set of service offerings and the ability to eventually expand the range of customers to include new markets.

Says Chua, "So we did our second review in '99. We had been doing okay when we changed from Capacity-driven to

Market-driven. We saw the strength in our results. But when we saw these major, unexpected changes happening we started asking ourselves if we should still focus on the same model, or should we change? We were supposed to have a review in 2002, but because of the Asian financial crisis a lot of things had changed. It was time for us to look into all the fundamental assumptions. Our competitors were also beginning to imitate us because they saw how well we performed. As a result of going through the process a second time, we decided that if this new supply chain capability proved to be well received by the IT industry, one day we could have the same capability to serve other industries such as pharmaceuticals."

The strategic refocusing has enabled Teckwah to once again forge a new direction and new growth without having to abandon their existing skill base. They are simply building onto it to find profitable opportunities.

"So now we are a total solution provider. We offer complete solutions to customers. We take over the customers' responsibility in the area of supply-chain management. It's high value and they pay us for that. Now that's *totally* different from an ordinary, traditional printing and packaging company. But there is still a genetic connection between where we started and where we are now. We are still very much linked to printing and packaging. These are core competencies. But this new strategy gets us out of our old sandbox," Thomas Chua states.

"The business performance, the growth and the bottom line are all positive," he says. "In 1997, almost 100 percent of our business was printing and packaging. In 1998, the supply-chain business was 6 percent of the total business. In 1999, it was 19 percent; in 2000 it was 49 percent. So today, it is almost half and half. Last year our turnover, compared to 1999, almost doubled. The top line doubled from 70 million Singapore dollars (41 million U.S.) to 130 million (76 million U.S.). The bottom line doubled from 7 million to 14 million Singapore dollars."

Looking back he says, "We could have engaged a consultant from our industry, but we chose not to. DPI's tool is applicable to *all* industries. The DPI process emphasizes changing the rules and controlling your sandbox. This intrigued us very much and we have done that.

"Also," he concludes, "I think that this process is very complete. It is not difficult to apply or understand. It is a process that *teaches you to fish*; it doesn't give you a fish! It's our own input. At the end of the day, we feel it is *our work* and not that of a consultant. This makes implementation much easier. Through the DPI process, we changed our mindset. In the past, our slogan was *Good Printing For A Good Image.* Now our slogan is *Best People, Best Solution.* From the 'pre-DPI' time to the end of 2000, Teckwah's revenue has grown 250 percent. Along with an overall recovery in the Asian economy, and the absolute commitment and hard work of our people, DPI is a key catalyst of that growth."

11
The Strategy Cemetery

"The resting place of failed strategies."

This space in Chapter 11 is being reserved for future examples of companies that:

- do not have a clear and well articulated strategy that will change the game to their advantage.

- are satisfied to compete "adequately" and do not strive for supremacy.

- do not have a Strategic Filter to make decisions.

- do not understand their Areas of Excellence.

- do not know which products, customers, market segments, and geographic areas to emphasize more or emphasize less.

- do not have a short list of Critical Issues that they are managing that will make their strategy and vision materialize over time.

- cannot communicate all of the above to their employees, their Board of Directors, their shareholders, and the financial community.

A good example of these faults at work is the saga of Compaq and DEC.

When 1 + 1 = Minus 2

Are some Driving Forces inherently incompatible? The answer is yes. Witness Compaq. During the 1990s, under the direction of CEO Eckhard Pfeiffer, the company soared on its Product-driven strategy – "business PCs." The strategy was so successful that management convinced itself that it could run any computer company. So when Digital Equipment Corporation (DEC) ran into difficulties, Compaq jumped in and bought DEC outright. Compaq quickly discovered that it had become the owner of a company with a very different strategy – "complex information systems for corporations" – a concept driven by a market category. Instead of the relatively simple business of selling and distributing personal computers in different colored boxes, Compaq now found itself in the business of providing large, multitask computers that required proprietary software and ongoing service, elements that PCs don't need. Here were two very different *businesses* – and, unfortunately, with two conflicting Driving Forces and strategies. It doesn't matter how smart management thinks it is. If two Driving Forces are *inherently incompatible*, they will never be made to work together as one.

This conflict turned out to be fatal for Pfeiffer. Six months after the merger became official, the company announced earnings that were substantially below Wall Street's expectations. Pfeiffer was quickly ousted by the board's Chairman, Benjamin Rosen. At the press conference announcing the dismissal, Rosen stated, "Compaq's strategy is sound. Execution is the hang-up. We need to execute better." Compaq's customers thought otherwise. "I don't know what they stand for anymore," said one. In our view, Compaq had adopted an incoherent strategy. And just as its customers recognized Compaq's strategic incoherence, so did its employees. Thus, the reason for poor execution. People cannot be expected to execute a strategy well that is flawed from the word "go."

If you have any candidates of such companies please list them below. I will use them as examples in my next book.

12

How Competitive Supremacy Enhances Shareholder Value

"The strategy *is* the share price."

Many CEOs of public companies that we work with believe that their stock price is considerably undervalued. On the other hand, most financial analysts we speak with tell us that the stock price is reflective, at least in part, of the CEO's ability, or inability, to articulate a coherent strategy. Therefore, depending on what the market *hears*, their stock is rightly valued, undervalued, or possibly even *over*valued. Yet, none of these may reflect the real value of that company. What an interesting dichotomy!

Obviously, such a dichotomy would interest anyone involved in the field of strategy, and it did us. As a result, we set out to explore the roots of this paradox and we discovered some very interesting factors at work.

Different Strokes For Different Folks

The most interesting phenomenon we observed was that the CEO and the financial analyst have very different perceptions as to how a company should be valued.

Most CEOs believe that the financial analyst's sole preoccupation is a focus on the quarterly "numbers." Therefore, they expend all their time and energy on meeting analysts' short-term expectations and discussing the "numbers," current and future.

The analysts, on the other hand, tell us that the "numbers," as lagging indicators, are becoming less important in valuing businesses. Leading or *non-financial* indicators drive at least 35 percent of investors' portfolio decisions. And the element that concerns them the most? *Uncertainty!* The greater the uncertainty, the greater this percentage becomes. The more uncertainty that analysts and investors believe there is about the viability of the CEO's strategy, the more influence it has over their investment decisions, which directly impacts the stock price positively or negatively. As put forth by a sell side analyst:

> "Strategy formulation and execution is the most important leading indicator because in an environment where investors are prepared to discount a CEO's business model between ten and twenty times revenue, progress in relation to milestones is all investors have to make an assessment. Failure to meet even a small short-term target will often have a disproportionate effect on investors' perceptions as to the *long-term viability* of the model."

Ford is a current example. After almost twenty years of steady strategic and operational performance vis-à-vis its U.S. competitors, the company, under Jacques Nasser's leadership, faltered and Mr. Nasser was replaced as CEO by another Ford family member – Bill Ford. In an attempt to reassure the financial community and boost his company's stock, Mr. Ford had a press conference with market analysts. The meeting backfired. Even though he correctly assessed that the problem stemmed from Ford's meandering from its

Product-driven strategy, most of the analysts did not believe that Mr. Ford's restructuring plans were aggressive enough and their recommendations were against purchasing the stock. As a result, the stock floundered at $15, half the price it held only a few months before.

Our conclusion in light of the current volatile markets is that a company's leading indicators, namely its ability to identify, demonstrate, and communicate value creation through . . .

- its strategy and vision

- its growth platforms such as new product innovation

- acquisitions

- its management expertise and experience

- its understanding of the internal environment

- its understanding of the external environment

. . . are key differentiators for investors, almost irrespective of short-term performance. The greater the uncertainty in any of these areas, the greater the significance of leading indicators to investors' decision making.

In fact, most analysts we speak to give us almost identical lists of criteria that they use to decide whether or not to recommend investing in a given company.

The Investor's Decision Criteria

The following is a list of criteria, in order of importance, used by financial analysts and fund managers:

- CEO's ability to articulate a clear strategy and vision and stick to it

- CEO's ability to get his executive team to commit to rapid and effective implementation of that strategy

- The company's market position vis-à-vis its competitors

- Management's credibility within the financial community

- Management's experience base

- The company's pace of new product creation and commercialization

- The company's investment in R&D versus that of its competitors

- The company's operational effectiveness

- The company's global reach

- The quality of its personnel

Yet, many CEOs have told us that in spite of the list above, large investors invest solely because of a CEO's ability to "make the numbers."

The Value Gap

Whatever the criteria used, the perception of many CEOs is that there is a gap between the market value of the company as seen by the financial community and the intrinsic value potential the CEO and the executive team believe the company has. Is the gap real? If so, how can it be quantified and effectively closed to achieve the value potential that the CEO *believes* the company has?

Competitive Supremacy Closes The Gap

At DPI, we feel strongly that using the *Strategic Thinking Process* to create a strategy that breeds *competitive supremacy* is the best way to enhance shareholder value and close the gap. Don Fites, CEO of Caterpillar through the 1990s, agrees: "If you want to maintain your leadership or even survive, the DPI process is the best I've seen. The creation of shareholder value has been rather spectacular!" Such a strategy increases the multiple on the stock price to a level higher than that of your peers.

The DPI process enables a company to develop a strategy that increases *real* value and then enables the CEO to clearly articulate it in a manner that communicates to the financial community *how* and *why* it will do so.

OMG: The Proof Is In The Pudding

Jim Mooney, CEO of OM Group (OMG-NYSE) in Cleveland, Ohio, rarely uses any "numbers" with the analysts that attend his quarterly briefing sessions. He does, however, utilize a lot of the outputs that were derived from our *Strategic Thinking Process.*

The following are excerpts from a recent interview explaining his approach.

How Vision Attracts Investment

"We've been well received by the markets for two reasons. The first is that we've been able to communicate our strategy in a way that the market can understand. The second is that we've delivered on that strategy. Without DPI's *Strategic Thinking Process,* that story would not have been as clear.

"The easiest way to describe our business is with the concepts developed during the *Strategic Thinking* work sessions. The best thing about it is that you don't have to give away your secrets, but you *do* let them know how you think. The financial community knows that they're buying a metal-based, specialty chemical company with strong growth opportunities. It's real simple. That's what we are.

"They know that we have a global presence. They know that we have ongoing product development, that we have an advanced and proprietary production capability.

"They know that they're buying into a company with experienced management that understands both the external environment as well as the internal one. They understand how we focus on niche markets and what areas we want to pursue and which ones we don't, based on our Strategic Profile. They know into which areas we want to expand our product portfolio. They know what our new product targets are and that acquisitions have to fit our Strategic Filter and the criteria it contains.

"The investors can see that we have absolute discipline in our focus and that there's no deviation from that. They don't want a public relations firm telling them what OMG is doing, they want to hear it direct.

"Too many companies suffer from a lack of vision and a distinctive strategy that sets them apart from their competitors. This hurts their chances of growing and impedes their ability to convince potential investors and customers that the company will grow. Relying on 'spin doctors' to position the company is no substitute for a CEO.

"I'll go to presentations and someone will be talking about how important their investor relations or public relations department is. And I'm sitting there thinking: 'My God, if you've got to talk about that, you've forgotten what you're in business for. You don't have a vision or strategy and you're trying to 'spin' one where there isn't any.

"Investors will support you with a clear vision. They won't support you if all you have is a public relations manager. I see good companies with solid technologies, solid production capabilities, and solid marketing skills but whose executives can't deliver a strategy and vision that will bring customer or shareholder satisfaction. Even if you have all these fundamentals in place, if customers and investors *don't understand your strategy*, they'll be reluctant to follow and support you.

"In eight years, OMG's stock has risen sevenfold, growing our market cap from $150 million to nearly $2 billion. Our revenues have grown 26 percent and our earnings 17 percent compounded annually. All this in a so-called commodity, no-growth, mature-market, low-price, low-margin business. We couldn't have done it without DPI's *Strategic Thinking Process.*"

Our experience would corroborate Jim Mooney's. In our view, the value gap perceived by most companies is caused largely by the CEO's inability to communicate the strategy to the financial community.

The following is a view of this phenomenon by
Deborah K. Pawlowski, President and CEO of Kei
Advisors, a Buffalo, New York consulting firm.
Kei specializes in assisting CEOs in communicating
effectively with the financial community to bridge
the value gap.

Closing The Value Gap

Investor relations is a value creation process. The content,
quality, depth, and consistency of the information provided by
companies to investors and potential investors promote market efficiency and manage expectations for future potential.
The value that investor relations can generate may be 'missing
value,' or value that is left unrecognized because the market
does not understand the future prospects for a company.
Additionally, IR can generate 'premium value,' or the incremental value a company creates by reducing its risk premium
when it provides markets with a greater understanding of its
potential relative to alternative investments. The following are
some practical methods you can implement that will enable
you to move your company up the premium value curve.

Are You Missing A Value Creation Opportunity?

A value gap exists when the market must rely on insufficient
information in its efforts to determine a company's future
cash flow potential, its risk, and its return opportunities.
Without a clear understanding of a company's strategy or
without a sense of the capability of the organization to deploy
that strategy, the market's assessment of value will very likely
be less than the true intrinsic value that may exist.

Value is the product of a financial equation that is developed
with many assumptions and interpretations. The market's
perceptions of a company's strategy, management capability,
capacity, and creativeness play into those assumptions, as
do the prevailing perceptions of the competitive landscape,
the strategic *opportunities*, and where your company fits in
the picture. If you do not clearly articulate your strategy and

it cannot be translated into financial outcome, or if what you do and say are not consistent, then the market by default has to use short-term proof points, such as quarterly earnings, to determine whether or not you are on track with the market's resulting expectations for your future. This leads to the destructive quarter-to-quarter 'earnings versus estimates' cycle, which forces executive management into short-term decision making, ultimately undermining a company's true performance potential.

Addressing The Value Gap Is A Value Creation Proposition

A Strategic Investor Relations program will effectively capture the components and magnitude of the value gap in order to close it. Resources – with executive management time being a major component – can be directed in a more efficient manner. Two objectives are therefore accomplished: intrinsic value is recognized and it is achieved in an efficient manner.

By establishing four clearly identified goals, CEOs can define the intent and direction of their IR program and ensure integration with their public relations, marketing, and general corporate communications efforts. Value is achieved by effectively creating an integrated communications plan that goes much deeper than is commonly practiced.

First, achieving fair valuation should be a goal in itself. In order to achieve this, you need to understand where you stand relative to similar investments. Then you must determine how effective your strategy is at deriving value and how consistent your performance is at achieving expected returns on invested capital. The value drivers – financial and non-financial – must be understood and communicated. Qualitative comments combined with quantitative responses will tell you if market participants see you as being fairly valued or not, and what the components of the value gap are. A peer investment analysis and shareholder analysis are also useful in understanding your relative value and potential. Premium value relative to similar investments is achieved when risk is reduced through a clear understanding of future potential. This can only be accomplished through timely and accurate information, consistently supported through decision patterns and performance.

Second, CEOs and their IR teams should cultivate a proactive and positive relationship with the investment community. This means understanding their information needs, their decision making processes, their audience. It entails outreach and conditioning – highly iterative activities. Importantly, conversation with this constituency means a *two-way flow* of information. Regular feedback interviews conducted by a third party after major communications events will help you to know what is not being understood, and what you need to emphasize or clarify in your presentations and comments. Reviewing your shareholder analysis, defining the shareholder profile that is best suited for the type of investment you are, and targeting the right audience with which to spend your time will generate greater results and make the use of your time more efficient.

Third, foster a communication environment open to change and progress. Responsiveness, depth of understanding, clarity and frequency – all of which comprise IR competency – contribute to this open environment. This character or trait of a company should be found in all areas, whether dealing with institutional investors, individual investors, customers, suppliers, or employees. The market needs to have the sense and understanding of how a business will behave with changing currents and shifting winds. Do you have a process for responding to inquiries in a timely fashion? Can your designated spokespersons clearly address your strategy, products, and markets, and translate that into financial outcomes? Are you all telling the same story? Before you started talking did you ask the interests of the investor or analyst?

Finally, and most importantly, your goal should be to establish and maintain solid credibility in the marketplace. Clearly, this is easier said than done. Financial results and opportunities are what value is created from, that is, the ability to earn an expected return on invested capital. The understanding of the opportunities is the intent of IR. Without credibility, interpretations of your company's opportunities are left to the crystal ball of the market and discounted with a higher risk premium.

All in all, value is about a business's performance and prospects. However, the outlook can only be valued if communicated clearly, consistently, and to the right audience. Content, form, frequency, and, most importantly, credibility all contribute to providing the market with the information it needs to derive value through first understanding and then closing the value gap.

CEO Interview

David Hoover
Chairman, President & CEO
Ball Corporation

> **"We agreed to five Critical Issues.
> Once you've done that and given
> ownership to individual managers,
> that becomes how you behave."**
>
> *– David Hoover*

The name Ball has been associated with container-making since two of the five Ball brothers borrowed $200 from an uncle in 1880 to make wood-jacketed tin cans. The company grew, adding three more brothers *and* their most famous product – the Ball home canning jar – which the company produced and sold for about a century.

But since the early 1990s, the company has gone through a major transition, spinning off the jar-making business and a group of other businesses. Ball hasn't made those jars for a decade. In fact, Ball makes no glass containers at all.

What it does make are metal cans and plastic bottles. Lots of them. In fact, last year Ball made about thirty-two *billion* beer and soda cans, as well as food cans and plastic bottles. The container business now accounts for about $3.3 billion in sales, with about $400 million also coming from an aerospace subsidiary.

Ball got into those high volume container businesses through a series of acquisitions over time, as they also sold off other companies. As the new Ball took shape, management knew they were on the right track, but performance wasn't where they wanted it to be. They wanted to refine a strategy for growth, and they selected DPI's *Strategic Thinking Process* to catalyze their thinking.

Says CEO David Hoover, "In 1998, the year that we moved our corporate headquarters to Colorado from Indiana, we knew, of course, that the beer/beverage can business had consolidated, that we were at about 17 to 18 percent market share along with four or five other companies, and that there probably needed to be more consolidation. We knew either we had to try to make something happen or something might happen to us. So we acquired the can business that was owned by Reynolds Metals and doubled our size. Ball became the largest beer/beverage can maker in North America, and probably in the world, at that time. We make about 35 percent of the beer/beverage cans. That was a big lift because there were consolidation savings and so on.

"We had also entered the PET plastic bottle business. We had invested in China. The company was getting along but not doing real well. After we moved to Colorado and hired some folks, including our Vice President of Corporate Planning & Development, John Hayes, we thought that we were at a stage where we were getting better performance but we thought we really needed to take a look at the planning process that we used, and try to think about 'How do we move this thing forward?'

"It was then that we ran across one of Mike Robert's books

on *Strategic Thinking.* From that we made contact with Mark Thompson, one of the DPI Partners, and somewhat later, going on two years ago now, we went through the *Strategic Thinking Process* with Mark and have benefited a lot from that. At the same time, the company had been changing and our management was changing. I became CEO in January 2001, was Chief Operating Officer before that, and was an advocate of this kind of strategy approach. We had other changes with the management, some new people, others who were doing new jobs. So it was a good time to make the critical thinking assessment. It allowed us to make sure that we aired all relevant points and talked freely and openly, so we could decide where to go in a structured way."

What most interested the Ball team about the DPI method was the concept of enabling the company's own people to contribute their ideas and experience, and develop a strategy they could agree on and, more importantly, gain ownership of that strategy.

"I think what attracted us first, just reading the book, is that DPI's process is based on clear thinking. What you don't get with DPI is some grey-headed guys who come in from a consulting firm who sell you the job and then send all the kids out to take your watch and tell you what time it is. We didn't need an army of people crawling around. It wasn't that we were in deep trouble, but it was that we wanted to get better. We knew that *we* had to do it.

"So I think the great thing about the DPI process is that it's largely a facilitation. A lot of it is done by example. It creates understanding. It gives the facilitator an interesting way of saying to you, 'Okay guys, what are you going to do? Here's one way to think about it. Let's identify what your core capabilities are, what the critical factors affecting your business are and what the issues that come out of that are.' It just resonated with us. So we had a group of close to thirty Ball people across the disciplines."

The process enabled Ball's managers to assess the company's current profile and to understand their current Business Concept and environment in order to make specific decisions about where they wanted to take the company in the future and how to create new opportunities for growth. Among the decisions central to creating that picture of the future was gaining agreement on the company's Future Driving Force.

Two of the choices they considered were Production Capacity or Product. Under the Production Capacity scenario, the company would strive to maximize capacity utilization by finding additional products, possibly unrelated to present products or markets, to keep the plants "full." A case could be made for this, and was. A more obvious choice would be Product-driven – metal cans and plastic bottles. After all, the company was among the world leaders in both categories. Yet, after intense debate and playing out the future scenarios for each, they came to the conclusion that a third choice, Market Category, best built upon their current capabilities, while creating new growth opportunities through innovative new products and processes.

As Hoover explains, "As the facilitator, Mark helped us to understand the difference between these different Driving Forces. He showed us examples of companies with different Driving Forces and how that shaped their businesses. He guided us through that very well. If you read our Business Concept, it says, basically, what we are – *We're a supplier of metal and plastic packaging products to food and beverage manufacturers.* And so we decided to focus on that market concept, which is a different answer than one might have expected and opens up new avenues to explore beyond our current products."

The key implication of that decision is the concentration of effort on cultivating the Areas of Excellence implied by a Market Category-driven strategy that all revolve around understanding and serving a specific set of needs of a market – in Ball's case, food and beverage companies that have an ongoing need for innovative packaging solutions.

"As a result, we have dedicated more resources to understanding where our customer is going," says Hoover. "We think that's where we've got to follow, and it's our lifeblood so we need to understand what they're doing. The whole idea is trying to think through – *What is our customer doing? Where is the market going to go? And what do we need to do to improve our performance and capability? Do we need new products? If so, what should they be? Should we get into a new kind of business and how would we do that?* I know that people here now think about these things a lot. I think the DPI process has helped us get focused and, in an organized way, consider all the relevant facts and factors in reaching a conclusion about what we should do. If I were to sum it up, it helped to get our management team on the same page. When you spend these few days together in an intense environment and you break into teams, it fosters communication about the things that are important. It also helps newer people become part of the team much quicker."

Out of the process, the Ball management group outlined what they now call "Five Keys to Success" to help communicate the basic principles of the new strategy to people throughout the company.

Hoover explains, "These five keys come right out of the DPI process. The first is to be close to our customers to understand their needs and their future direction and what they're trying to do. And it's all the way up and down the organization, from the senior management to the people on the manufacturing floor in our plants.

"The second is this whole idea of creativity and imagination. And that's where DPI's *Strategic Product Innovation Process* comes in. And we're taking advantage of that to create new products, new processes, and new businesses.

"Third is attention to detail. We tend to be relentless at managing our business. At Ball that starts with housekeeping. I mean you could eat off the floor in one of our can plants and we don't have any janitors. We think that's where it starts. And then you manage the entire operation like that to yield high productivity and low cost."

"The fourth key is to build on our strengths, which is where a lot of the DPI process comes in – our historic strengths of high quality and greatest value to the customer, and to couple that with this rigorous approach to managing the business.

"Finally, and I saved the most important for last, we want to behave as owners. I talk a lot about that. We expect our employees to act like true owners of the business. What does that mean? Well, it means you show up when you're needed and you go home when the work's done. It means that you care so much that you don't want any customer to be disappointed, that you care about the other people in the business because they're your co-owners. I want you to think this is your place. And that's a powerful thing. And actually if everybody behaves like an owner, those other things that I talked about, they're going to happen."

The part of the process that converts those conceptual goals into tangible actions is the development of a list of Critical Issues that are assigned to individuals to manage to completion.

"We agreed to five Critical Issues," Hoover recalls. "Once you've done that and given ownership to individual managers, that becomes how you *behave*."

A few months later, with those issues well on their way to completion, top management again met with DPI to refine the strategy. The result was a slight redefinition of the business concept and a couple of new Critical Issues.

"Before we would have said we were only a supplier of rigid metal and plastic packaging. We decided the containers don't necessarily have to be rigid. It's subtle, but it opens up new opportunities. We also added an important Critical Issue – innovation – new products, new concepts, which led to us using DPI's *Strategic Product Innovation Process*. We've done that two or three times and come up with eleven excellent ideas to work on."

Ball found that the *SPI Process* was a more structured approach to product development than they were accustomed to.

"Most ideas before had been based on an engineer's idea of something he could make, but the customer wouldn't necessarily want or need. Since we are much more focused on our customers and where they and their markets are going, we now have a process in place that helps us turn that knowledge into successful new products. It helped bring order to what most of us think of as chaos."

The results over the past couple of years are impressive and Ball executives now feel their strategy – understanding their customers' needs and providing innovative new products – is a key component in their growth.

"We've grown in the food can business for example. We've grown that business in a flat market, not by cutting prices and taking other people's business, but by finding new applications, by having customers who are growing. We grow right along with them. Those are some of the reasons we're doing well."

Well indeed. Even in the bear market of 2001 to 2002, Ball has received a vote of confidence from the market, with its share price *tripling* in about a year.

The Ball, as they say, is rolling.

CEO Interview

Greg Tunney
President & Chief Operating Officer
Phoenix Footwear Group

> **"We're the number one performing
> footwear stock this year . . .
> The DPI process doesn't do all this *for* you . . .
> *We* have to do it . . . *We're* the engines."**
>
> *– Greg Tunney*

Daniel Green Footwear was in deep trouble. It was 1998 and the company had been losing money for several years, with sales limping along at about $14 million and its stock hovering around $2. Saddled with antiquated factories, a highly seasonal women's slipper line, and a mountain of debt, the company was sinking fast.

Today, a little over three years later, it's a very different story. Sales are near $40 million and growing, and earnings are strong. The company's stock, one of the few bright lights on NASDAQ in 2001 and recently listed on AMEX (symbol PXG), *tripled* in a year. The company has been resurrected from its near-death experience through a series of smart, gutsy strategic decisions and has recently taken a new name – Phoenix Footwear Group, which aptly symbolizes the transformation.

Getting to this point hasn't been easy. As a first step toward recovery, Chairman and CEO Jim Riedman decided to bring in Greg Tunney – who he knew had a successful track record of turnarounds in the footwear business – as President and COO. When Tunney arrived in 1998, he immediately recognized some fundamental problems, based on prior experience in the shoe business. Knowing that Daniel Green's business model, reliant on domestic manufacturing in the United States, was obsolete, he began the difficult task of steering the company toward a model based on outsourcing. That would ultimately mean closing three plants and completely revamping the company top to bottom. After about a year of "cleaning house," he brought in DPI's *Strategic Thinking Process* to enable his managers to understand the future they faced and forge a strategy they would understand and, most importantly, support.

As Greg Tunney recalls, "When I got here the business was in a major crisis situation. It hadn't made a profit in several years and I was brought in to help turn it around."

His last assignment in the footwear industry had led him to deal successfully with many of the same problems that had brought Daniel Green to near bankruptcy. He knew, coming in, basically what needed to be done. The economics of the industry had made the manufacture of footwear in the United States all but impossible. The cost of operating its three plants was literally killing them.

"The first year at Daniel Green was damage control, figuring out how many cracks there were in the Titanic and putting together a new senior management team. Then after we determined everything that had to be done, the second year we started to make some changes and brought in DPI."

Now, with a strong handle on the situation, DPI's *Strategic Thinking Process* would help to solidify the management group's thinking behind what was for them a completely new approach to doing business – getting out of manufacturing altogether, transitioning to an "outsourced" operation.

Says Tunney, "I saw DPI as a way of really getting buy-in from the team standpoint, of having them *understand* the vision, not to have it be *my* vision. To have them all be part of that vision, to me, was worth its weight in gold."

DPI Partner Craig Bowers facilitated the process. Says Tunney of the facilitator's role, "I think the facilitator is critical, especially in the initial phase. If I were to try and lead it there'd be no credibility to the process. They'd all say, 'Okay Greg, what is it *you* want us to do here?' The facilitator really opens up the minds of the participants and says 'Okay, this is *your* process. What do you want the company to be?' And as a facilitator Craig has the process knowledge and enough experience at this to open up the whole can of worms and bring it to a conclusion."

As the process progressed, it enabled the participants to develop a complete picture of the company – and how it had gotten into this dire situation. In effect, Green had been operating under a Production Capacity Driving Force, doing whatever it could to try to keep its factories operating at capacity. But the cost of keeping the aging factories open far exceeded the revenue they produced. After bringing all the facts out into the light, it didn't take long for the group to come to the realization that this model was no longer viable, and that a shift to a Product/Concept Driving Force was the only path that made sense.

"As we started to clarify the discussion, it became obvious to everyone, whether you were on the manufacturing side or whatever area you worked in, that if we were going to survive, we were going to have to become a Product-driven company," says Tunney. "We had been very Manufacturing-driven. That was what drove Daniel Green for 120 years. You had this silo called a factory. You had to keep it chugging 24/7 to cover overhead. That's what everyone lived and died for. But the economics of that hadn't worked in many years. So we decided we had to make this major change. Today it's no longer, 'Keep the factory going.' Now it's, 'Let's make the right product at the right time at the right price so we can make money.' And it had been a long time since the company made money. So it really changed the whole concept of what was going to drive our company. What's driving us now is delivering the best products. Before, we didn't care what kind of widget we made as long as we kept the factory full. That's a huge change."

Out of the process came a new unity of purpose behind a clear Business Concept that would provide a strategic filter for the coming years:

> Daniel Green's strategy is to develop and market slipper-designed footwear. We will strive to offer value-added, distinctive products that are tailored to the needs of the end users of high potential and growing mid- to top-tier channels where we can leverage our slipper technologies.

Noticeably absent from this statement is any mention of manufacturing, which would now be completely outsourced. Inherent in this new Product/Concept-driven strategy would be new Areas of Excellence – Product Development, Market Awareness, and Sales Relationship Building.

In what would at first be an uphill battle, the company set out to resolve the list of Critical Issues set out during the process to accomplish the next phase of its strategic renaissance – complete transformation from domestic manufacturer to "completely sourced operation," with new products to generate profitable sales and growth.

Making these essential changes depended on the support of the Board and its Chairman. Says Tunney, "Our Chairman and our Board of Directors were instrumental in our company's change of direction because they were willing to support the management team in making a long-term change in our direction. Most boards are not willing to give up short-term profits for long-term growth."

To make a long story much shorter, the company's plants were divested by the end of 1999, and manufacturing of its products outsourced to new partners in other locations, such as Brazil, where high quality products could be produced competitively. Similarly, design was transferred to a variety of partners who could provide new products for the pipeline to keep consumer interest fresh. Its retail relationships changed significantly in line with its new strategy, concentrating on higher end distribution channels like department stores as opposed to low end discount chains, and getting out of its money-losing private label business altogether.

Things began to improve despite some difficult times in the retail industry, and Green was eventually able to acquire two companies. The first was L.B. Evans, which brought in a line of men's slippers, rounding out the slipper line. Next was Penobscot Shoe Company of Old Town, Maine, which contributed two well-established brands of women's "comfort" shoes, Trotters and SoftWalk. Penobscot was also a comfortable fit with Daniel Green since they were already a completely outsourced firm.

Ultimately, Daniel Green moved its main offices to Old Town, and decided to sell the slipper business in an effort to concentrate on less seasonal and more profitable segments. The sale provided enough cash to retire nearly all of the company's debt and gave it flexibility to grow. The sale of the Daniel Green brand also necessitated a change in name. Phoenix Footwear Group, as the company is now known, was appropriately selected.

But all that change in the business had also meant major changes in personnel – including people who had been recruited over those two years and those who came in through the Penobscot acquisition. So it was time, once again, to bring in DPI to review the strategy and unify the largely new group. The process allowed the participants, most of them for the first time, to see the company as a whole, and so to understand how the pieces fit together to support the Product/Concept Driving Force.

"During the process, we found out that 80 percent of our managers really didn't understand what we did as a company," Tunney recounts. "They each knew their own world – say, the Credit Department or Customer Service Department, and what they each did day to day. They didn't realize that the concept of the company is really to develop, design, and deliver footwear products. That's not surprising because so much of that doesn't happen here in Old Town. Production is in Brazil. Our designers are all over the country. Our technical team is offshore. We're more of a processing area here. These products show up in a container every day and are shipped out to other places. So their concept was generally more oriented to the paperwork all this involved and not toward being Product-driven. They never realized that the reason we have all these departments is really to support the Product and Sales teams. Products and Sales were probably viewed as more of an annoyance. The process enabled everyone to see, 'Hey, that's what really butters our bread.' The experience of looking at the whole company through the DPI process was an eye-opening experience for them."

The result is a slightly revamped strategy – featuring "footwear," not slippers, with an optimum combination of comfort and fit – and an organization that now fully understands that strategic direction.

A new Business Concept broadens the product possibilities, yet clearly defines the types of products and markets, as well as Areas of Excellence, it will pursue:

> Phoenix Footwear Group's strategy will be to develop, market, and service quality footwear. We will focus on growth-oriented customers and consumers, in the moderate to better price footwear category. We will grow by concentrating on geographic markets where we can leverage our superior design sourcing techniques as it applies to styling, comfort, and fit technologies. We will accomplish these objectives by focusing our sales and marketing efforts within established channels of distribution.

The key benefit to going through the process again, though, was the unification of an organization that had undergone massive change in a short period of time.

As Tunney explains, "I think, as a result of going through the process that second time, that we're much more cross-functional now. Before, I think there were boundaries around departments. There's more of a spirit of 'Now I understand what you guys have to get done. So how can I support you in doing that?' As a result, I think our flexibility as a company has greatly improved. There are challenges every day. Having this improved understanding and communication has made us more fluid as an organization. When a problem comes up, our managers can get together and say, 'Okay, now what can each department do to attack this situation and solve it?'"

Today, Phoenix Footwear is a far different and much better company than it was only a few years ago. A look at the financial situation confirms that emphatically.

"For the first quarter this year, earnings are up," says Tunney. "They tripled in the first quarter. We're the *number one* performing footwear stock in the stock market this year, the *number one* performing stock with regard to sales and revenues and increased earnings. So the DPI process is great, but the bottom line is the results it helped us achieve.

"The DPI process doesn't do all this *for* you. Maybe that's what is so good about it. *We* have to do it; *we're* the engine. DPI may be the gasoline in the engine, but *we* had to get the engine right. We had to get a lot of things in place. We had ten or twelve managers in here and a lot of different ideas of what the vision was. When we finished the process, everybody was on the same page. And I've been pleased to see some managers coming out of their shells and achieving their potential. That comes from a feeling that, 'I can make a difference,' – not just going along with this vision, but being a part of it. It makes my job a lot easier. They know the vision. It's on paper. It's in their minds.

"We were looking for a way to bring this team together, how to get a focus on the strategy, to get everybody marching to the same tune. And the DPI process was definitely the glue that brought it together and solidified it. Without it, I think we could have had some decent results, but this really expedited the process. I think this increased the velocity in which the team came together. It's created a culture here and we truly do have a culture in the company now. We have managers here now who understand that culture and believe in it and it works."

13

CEOs Validate the Process

"The answers to your strategic questions exist in the minds of your own management team."

– Jack Messman

Over the years, DPI has worked with the CEOs of over four hundred companies worldwide. During this time, third party interviews have been conducted with many of them to obtain feedback about our concepts and processes. We discovered two interesting things as a result. In one respect, they all experienced the same thing – the *Strategic Thinking Process* produced strategies that their management teams could agree on and implement effectively – and that gave them supremacy over their competitors. What was *different* about them is that they all had a different "need" or problem to solve, and thus experienced a wide variety of benefits unique to them.

The following short excerpts illustrate the many beneficial effects of this powerful process from the point of view of your peers – the CEOs of major companies from a wide range of industries.

Achieving Agreement, Ownership, And Commitment

"No matter what you think, you need to do this. This will change the way you look at your business. This will not only change how you look at the future, but also how your key managers do. They will have the same vision you have. This is the key to succeeding."

Gilles Labbé, Chairman & CEO, Héroux, Inc.

"We liked the DPI approach because it draws on the knowledge and experience of our people rather than attempting, as some consulting firms tend to, to convince us of their view of the future and how they would position the company.

"We owe a debt of gratitude to DPI. DPI had the right process at the right time for NorAm. NorAm is not the same company that it was when we began the DPI Process."

Milt Honea, Chairman, President & CEO
NorAm Energy Corporation

"I chose this process because I liked its practical approach. It was not geared to having somebody come in and tell you what to do. DPI took us through a process of arriving at mutually agreed upon priorities. This process creates momentum and leads to an action agenda that is carried out."

Ted Hutton, President & CEO, Waverly, Inc.

"The great thing about this process was that we had input from a lot of different folks. They were all able to contribute, and this created a deep sense of ownership. We're very pleased with our progress. I think when you achieve ownership through

broad participation in creating strategy, you get tremendous commitment from everyone within the organization."
James N. Plato, President & CEO
United Presidential Life Insurance Company

"In the first two to three hours of the meeting with DPI, I was astonished that our senior management group had no concept of our strategy, and disagreed with it once they learned of it! I was happy about DPI's intervention because, at the conclusion, we all knew and agreed with our strategy – there was absolutely no question about our beliefs and direction."
Gary Holland, President & CEO
DataCard Corporation

"The single best thing to come out of this from Carlson's perspective is that our entire management team has now been able to define what we are, agree on what we need to do to build on our unique production capabilities, and focus our energies on making them happen."
H. L. Kephart, CEO, G. O. Carlson, Inc.

"I was really looking for something that would force our people to think and come up with some answers. It did bring us much closer and the team definitely functioned much better. It gave us consensus. It led us to focus on a few Critical Issues. It led the whole group to take on ownership."
Rafaël Decaluwé, CEO, N. V. Bekaert, S.A.

Strategic Thinking vs. Other Strategy Creation Methods

"The whole idea of someone from the outside telling people who have spent their whole life in a company, that something will or won't work, is not really a good idea. They don't have the insight into what makes the company tick. The thing this process does very well, and I've seen it done over and over, is it forces you to find the answers to these issues yourself."
Don Fites, CEO, Caterpillar, Inc. (1990 – 1999)

"We went through a number of consultants who worked with us. Among several others, we had the top strategy consultants at the time, Michael Porter, and Noel Tichy who had worked with General Electric on their break-out process . . . Rather than spending two or three years getting the background that a traditional strategy consultant like Porter might have wanted, we felt the DPI process was a much more straightforward approach that we would be comfortable with and get faster results, which at the time was important."
Glen Barton, CEO, Caterpillar, Inc. (1999 – Present)

"Some consultants come in and pick everyone's brains and put on paper what they *think* everyone *thinks*. But you try to push that down to people and it's not *their* strategy. It's what someone *else* thinks is their strategy. DPI's way works much better."
Serge Bragdon, CEO, Uniboard Canada, Inc.

"In my corporate background at General Motors, Moog (an aerospace company), and Sperry Corporation, we were involved in all kinds of traditional strategic planning methods, like the Boston Consulting Group and PIMS, etc. DPI's approach is a *thinking* process that allows you to continually modify and change. It puts a thinking process into the hands of real-world operations people. And that's the way to get strategic advantage, from my point of view."
Tony Raimondo, CEO
Behlen Manufacturing Company

"The rational approach, the process, and the fact that results could be realized in a compact period of time really appealed to me."
Dennis F. Truss, President & CEO
British Columbia Buildings Corporation

"The *Strategic Thinking Process* puts the emphasis on thinking versus planning. Some consultants actually develop a plan, deliver it to you, and tell you that's the plan you ought

to execute. DPI didn't do that. They provided a thinking process that enabled us to create the strategy ourselves. I think every organization, no matter what the size, could really benefit from going through DPI's process. It gets to the heart of the fundamental issues that are driving the organization."
Robert Evans, CEO, Material Sciences Corporation

"The thing I like about the DPI process is the strategic thinking. It's not a complex strategic planning process. It allows you to identify the Critical Issues in your business. It gives you a method of addressing them. You're dealing with the *concept* of your business and how you want to go about business, instead of all the numbers. It becomes a vital part of your operations. You don't just put it on the shelf and wait until the next planning period."
Craig Smith, CEO, Raytech Corporation

The Concept Of Driving Force

"One of the most powerful aspects of *Strategic Thinking* is the concept of Driving Force. Once you understand your Driving Force, you understand what makes your company unique. We then had a roadmap not only to what had to be done, but how to do it."
Carl Oberg, President, Sotreq, S.A.

"In that whole discussion, probably the single biggest discovery was this Driving Force concept. What is your Driving Force? Your Driving Force is the one thing you do better than anyone else, or the one thing that makes you unique. And identifying that Driving Force led us to the conclusion that that's what we needed to protect."
Mike Harnetty, Division Vice President
3M Corp., Protective Materials Division

"The *Strategic Thinking Process* walks everybody through a logical process that helps them reach a unified conclusion about the Driving Force that makes us unique as a business. It's surprising. Most of our people were betting that we would not come to a unified conclusion. Most of us believed that there was no common thread or Driving Force joining the units together. I was hoping that *Strategic Thinking* would bring out a common thread, and it did that marvelously well. I see the management team being able to sort through possible acquisitions much more easily. And that's because it's now easier to evaluate whether an acquisition will support or contribute to our Driving Force."

Tony Raimondo, CEO
Behlen Manufacturing Company

Immediate And Sustained Results

"We came out of those sessions with a clear action plan as to how we would get the necessary results. In all, we added $7 million in profit in the first year compared to the previous year's results. We were able to achieve fast results because everybody believed in the strategy and objectives. The combination of strategy development and strategy deployment is what is different about DPI, and what creates success."

Luc Desjardins, President & CEO
Mail-Well Envelope Division

"A key result is the best harmony we've ever had among our top thirty people. We have been able to crystallize real issues that we can get our teeth into and act on. Normally, consultants are a flash-in-the-pan. They're gone before you know it, and a lot of money has been spent for very little progress. With DPI, the longer you're with them, the better it is, which is quite rare. The more you use them, the more depth you're able to achieve in terms of using the processes to penetrate the organization."

Mark Ungerer, President & COO, FLEXcon, Inc.

"There's a commitment to the future beyond the coming quarter by people that had never thought strategically. The outgrowth of this new strategic thinking among our people is very apparent. For example, 50 percent of all our sales last year came from products that are less than eighteen months old. We just came off four straight quarters of record profits following a record year last year."

Odey Powers, CEO
Nicolet Instrument Corporation

"First you need to have an open mind when you go into this process. I suggest you read one of Mike Robert's books. If you find it interesting, and feel the *Strategic Thinking Process* might fit your operation, then you should put it into practice, because what you read in the book is really what happens! I was actually surprised, because usually when you read these types of books and do what they say, you don't get the results you thought you would. The process forced us to come up with the result without getting trapped in the 'How are we going to do it?' question. I think the DPI process is the only way to do that."

Jean Laflamme, President
South Shore Industries, Ltd.

"I think this process goes much further than others in terms of implementation. We don't want words on a paper gathering dust on a shelf. This *Strategic Thinking Process* gives you concrete actions to take and a plan to get them done. I think this process is terrific. It's straightforward. It concentrates the mind. Anybody can do this, any size business in my view, and benefit from the discipline."

Ron Eden, President & CEO
Canada Malting Company, Ltd.

"We are in a much better position to face a very difficult business and economic environment and the results are starting to show. In a stagnant market, we have increased our market share by 5 percent in twelve months because we have been implementing a cohesive plan derived from a clear strategy based on a unified vision of what our management wants GPV to become."

Michel Bouchon, CEO
Garnier Ponsonnet Vuillard (GPV) France

"The most beneficial output has been the increased communication and cooperation among our subsidiaries towards improved customer service, employee involvement and satisfaction, and achieving sustainable growth in shareholder value."

James Glasser, Chairman of the Board
President & CEO, GATX

"Going through it, nothing seemed like rocket science. It was just basic and logical. But it really made us think. It's common sense. It was quite different than your typical strategic planning. In the older strategic planning methods you tend to develop a bunch of paper and you put it in a big bound volume and it sits on a shelf. Our business could increase by double or more in the next couple of years because we now are able to focus on the priority issues and deal with them quickly."

John Halloran, CEO, D. B. Riley, Inc.

"As a CEO, I have always tried to build management teams, which are not the same as groups of managers. DPI serves as the 'aggregator element' that helps to form these managers into teams and enables them to combine their knowledge of the business to make decisions they will have to live with and implement. DPI's *Strategic Thinking Process* enabled our team to create a sound business strategy. The *e-Strategy Process* then allowed even our non-technical managers to build an Internet strategy that supports that strategy. Both are being implemented with excellent results."

Ilídio Silva, CEO, Radio Popular

Strategic Filter: Choosing The Right Opportunities

"We were spending our time on things we shouldn't spend our time on. In going through the *Strategic Thinking Process*, we now see clearly where we should put more and less emphasis."

Ray Rush, CEO, Canadian Insurance Management

"Using DPI's process, we developed a very successful strategy. It basically showed us that the answers to your strategic questions exist in the minds of your own management team. It gave us a unified strategy against which we could test our tactics on a day-to-day basis."
Jack Messman, CEO, Union Pacific Resources

"The DPI process brings greater discipline in establishing initiatives, and improving our prioritization. It has elevated the organization's confidence in being able to continue to produce exceptional results. We have a means to identify opportunities much more quickly and cast off pseudo opportunities more quickly and systematically than we could have in the past."
Mike Magsig, Former CEO,
Cologne Life Reinsurance Company

Keeping The New Product Hopper Full

"Using DPI's *Strategic Thinking Process* and *Strategic Product Innovation Process*, we created a sound corporate strategy and a permanent attitude of innovation. This has contributed decisively to our ability to leverage our capacity to generate new business and penetrate new markets through the launching of new products and the development of new manufacturing processes. This new attitude brought visible changes in the culture of the company and increased our people's motivation. This has improved our efficiency with strong impact on our results. Vicaima now has the necessary processes to open the doors of excellence."
Arlindo Leite, CEO, Vicaima Industria

"What we have now is a systematic process to create new products and make innovation happen on our own. In the next five years, these new products will result in sales above nineteen billion escudos ($100 million U.S.) with costs that will not exceed twelve billion escudos ($63 million U.S.). The richness of the decisions – exclusively ours – has led to an

implementation with results unexpectedly higher than those that we were used to."
Carlos Sousa Alves, CEO, TELEPAC

The Process Facilitator: Essential To Success

"I would like to say a word about the need for a third party, objective facilitator with a structured process. This role is indispensable. Otherwise the group and the discussion would meander all over the place."
Jesus Catania, Managing Director
FAGOR Electrodomésticos

"I believe, and of course it's been proven, that these DPI people are not consultants in the traditional sense, they're facilitators. And the process is what they offer. It's a wonderful process, and it really works. I think it's so flexible that it can work with a small corporate group or with the much broader group that we involved."
Vernon Oechsle, Chairman & CEO
Quanex Corporation

"The wonderful thing about this process is that a consultant didn't come in and tell us what our strategy should be. The facilitator of the process didn't tell us anything. He just kept directing our thinking, asking questions. And the great thing was, he would never give up. Even when we were getting tired or ducking an issue that was unresolved, he wouldn't let us duck. He just kept on directing us to get to a conclusion."
James Glasser, Chairman of the Board
President & CEO, GATX

"The fact that *you do the thinking yourselves* under the guidance of an experienced DPI facilitator is what makes the difference. The facilitator provides focus and know-how derived from having done it again and again, having previously brought disparate groups through the same process. A facilitator keeps the process moving, preventing it from going off on non-productive meanders."

Russell Luigs, Chairman, Global Marine, Inc.

Changing The Rules Of Play:

"We were a bit skeptical that we could come to a consensus with thirty managers participating. It's difficult enough to get consensus with five or six people sitting around a table . . . but we did come to a consensus and were very pleased with the result. We decided to change the rules of play in our market... now we're feeling the impact. It's an amazing change of direction."

Claude Lalonde, President, Groupe Cantrex, Inc.

"DPI has advanced the concept that you can make your *competitors irrelevant.* The process allows you to develop a vision and a strategy *that truly puts you in greater control of your own destiny,* and really allows you to spend much more time thinking about where *you* want to go, rather than what the *competition* is doing."

William S. Rafferty, Senior Vice President, Mestek, Inc.

"Every time we make an investment in technology, we ask ourselves to use some of Mike Robert's concepts – how will it help us change or influence the rules of play in our competitive sandbox? How can we leverage that Driving Force more effectively in terms of value to our customers and the information that we provide? It enables us to continue to differentiate ourselves and continue to add value. It allows us, as DPI says, to choose our competitors, to manage our competitors' strategies, to neutralize their Driving Force by changing the rules of play."

Bruce Simpson, CEO, FedEx Custom Critical

We hope that you have enjoyed this book and that you have found some ideas that will add value to your business. If we can be of assistance in helping you do this, please do not hesitate to give us a call.